GUILT-FREE
ITALIAN

GUILT-FREE
ITALIAN

eat well, be happy, and stay fit

Cook the Italian way without the fat: over 160 delicious, traditional
step-by-step recipes for long life and good health

Editor anne sheasby

southwater

This edition is published by Southwater,
an imprint of Anness Publishing Ltd, 108 Great Russell Street,
London WC1B 3NA; info@anness.com

www.southwaterbooks.com; www.annesspublishing.com;
twitter: @Anness_Books

If you like the images in this book and would like to investigate
using them for publishing, promotions or advertising, please visit
our website www.practicalpictures.com for more information.

© Anness Publishing Limited 2015

A CIP catalogue record for this book is available from
the British Library.

Publisher: Joanna Lorenz
Project Editor: Felicity Forster
Editor: Anne Sheasby
Nutritional Analysis: Jill Scott
Recipes: Catherine Atkinson, Carla Capalbo, Kit Chan, Jacqueline
Clarke, Maxine Clarke, Frances Cleary, Carol Clements, Roz Denny,
Matthew Drennan, Joanna Farrow, Christine France, Sarah Gates,
Shirley Gill, Carole Handslip, Christine Ingram, Patricia Lousada,
Norma MacMillan, Sue Maggs, Elizabeth Martin, Sarah Maxwell,
Janice Murfitt, Annie Nichols, Angela Nilsen, Maggie Pannell,
Louise Pickford, Jennie Shapter, Anne Sheasby, Hilaire Walden,
Laura Washburn, Steven Wheeler, Kate Whiteman, Judy Williams,
Elizabeth Wolf-Cohen, Jeni Wright
Photographers: Karl Adamson, Edward Allwright, David Armstrong,
Steve Baxter, Nicki Dowey, James Duncan, Michelle Garrett,
Amanda Heywood, Tim Hill, David Jordan, Dave King, Don Last,
Patrick McLeavey, Michael Michaels, Thomas Odulate, Peter Reilly,
William Lingwood
Designers: Nigel Partridge, Ian Sandom
Indexer: Helen Snaith
Production Controller: Pirong Wang

COOK'S NOTES
Bracketed terms are intended for American readers.
For all recipes, quantities are given in both metric and
imperial measures and, where appropriate, in standard cups
and spoons. Follow one set of measures, but not a mixture,
because they are not interchangeable.
Standard spoon and cup measures are level.
1 tsp = 5ml, 1 tbsp = 15ml, 1 cup = 250ml/8fl oz.
Australian standard tablespoons are 20ml. Australian readers
should use 3 tsp in place of 1 tbsp for measuring small quantities.
American pints are 16fl oz/2 cups. American readers should use
20fl oz/2.5 cups in place of 1 pint when measuring liquids.
Electric oven temperatures in this book are for conventional ovens.
When using a fan oven, the temperature will probably need to be
reduced by about 10–20°C/20–40°F. Since ovens vary, you should
check with your manufacturer's instruction book for guidance.
The nutritional analysis given for each recipe is calculated per
portion (i.e. serving or item), unless otherwise stated. If the recipe
gives a range, such as Serves 4–6, then the nutritional analysis will
be for the smaller portion size, i.e. 6 servings. The analysis does not
include optional ingredients, such as salt added to taste.
Medium (US large) eggs are used unless otherwise stated.

PUBLISHER'S NOTE
Although the advice and information in this book are believed to be
accurate and true at the time of going to press, neither the authors
nor the publisher can accept any legal responsibility or liability for
any errors or omissions that may have been made nor for any
inaccuracies nor for any loss, harm or injury that comes about from
following instructions or advice in this book.

CONTENTS

INTRODUCTION

Italians are passionate about their food and always enjoy spending time preparing, cooking and eating food with family and friends. Food is one of their greatest pleasures and Italians are fortunate to be able to enjoy many regional variations in the food and dishes they eat. Italian food is thought by many of us to be laden with calories and fat, but in fact the same appealing scope and variety of flavours from Italy can be enjoyed as part of a healthy, low-fat cuisine.

Many traditional Italian foods such as the abundance of fresh Mediterranean sun-ripened vegetables, fresh herbs and many different types of pasta are naturally low in fat, making them ideal to enjoy as part of a low-fat eating plan. Quality and freshness of foods are both of great importance to the Italians and much of the fresh produce eaten in Italy is grown or produced locally. When it comes to cooking foods such as vegetables, they are often cooked in simple ways to bring out their delicious and natural flavours.

Olive oil is the primary fat used for cooking in Italy and it is also commonly used for dressing foods such as salads. Olive oil is a "healthier" type of fat which is high in monounsaturated fat and low in saturated fat and so long as it is used in moderation, it can also be enjoyed as part of a low-fat diet.

Some other typical Italian ingredients, such as pancetta, salami, Parmesan and mozzarella, are high in fat but are easily substituted with lower-fat foods such as lean bacon and reduced-fat mozzarella, or, in many recipes, the quantity of the high-fat food can often simply be reduced to lower the fat content of the dish.

BELOW: Italian food is packed with flavour and colour, and can be amazingly low in fat too.

ABOVE: Pasta, rice, olive oil, nuts, cheese, meat, olives, garlic, and fresh fruit and vegetables can all be enjoyed as part of a low-fat Italian diet.

In Italy, pasta and rice dishes form a large part of the cuisine and both are ideal for a low-fat diet as they are naturally high in carbohydrates and low in fat, so long as the sauce served with the pasta or the other ingredients used for a rice dish such as a risotto are also low in fat!

Most of us eat fats in some form or another every day and we all need a small amount of fat in our diet to maintain a healthy, balanced eating plan. However, most of us eat far too much fat and we should all be looking to reduce our overall fat intake, especially saturated fats.

Weight for weight, dietary fats supply far more energy than all the other nutrients in our diet and if you eat a diet that is high in fat but don't exercise sufficiently to use up that energy, you will gain weight.

By cutting down on the amount of fat you eat and making easy changes to your diet, such as choosing the right types of fat, using low-fat and fat-free products whenever possible and making simple changes to the way you prepare and cook food, you will soon be reducing your overall fat intake and enjoying a much healthier lifestyle – and you'll hardly notice the difference!

As you will see from this cookbook, it is certainly practicable to eat and enjoy Italian food as part of a low-fat eating plan. We include lots of useful and informative advice, including an introduction to basic healthy eating guidelines; helpful hints and tips on low-fat and fat-free ingredients and low-fat or fat-free cooking techniques; practical tips on how to reduce fat and saturated fat in your diet; an interesting insight into the traditional Italian kitchen and the types of ingredients and foods most commonly used in everyday Italian cooking, as well as an appealing selection of over 160 delicious and easy-to-follow low-fat Italian recipes for all the family to enjoy.

Each recipe includes a nutritional breakdown, providing at-a-glance calorie and fat contents per serving. All the recipes in this cookbook are very low in fat – each containing five grams of fat or less per serving, some containing less than one gram of fat per serving.

You will be surprised and delighted at this tempting collection of recipes which ranges from soups, appetizers and salads to main-course pasta dishes, breads and desserts. All the recipes contain less fat than similar traditional Italian recipes and yet they are packed full of Italian flavour and appeal. This practical cookbook will give you a valuable insight into low-fat and Italian cookery and will enable you to enjoy Italian food that is healthy, delicious and nutritious as well as being low in fat.

BELOW: Fresh fruits are an ideal choice for fat-free cooking because they are naturally low in fat. They can be used in both sweet and savoury Italian dishes.

HEALTHY EATING GUIDELINES

A healthy diet is one that provides us with all the nutrients we need. By eating the right types, balance and proportions of foods, we are more likely to feel healthy, have plenty of energy and a higher resistance to disease that will help prevent us from developing illnesses such as heart disease, cancers, bowel disorders and obesity.

By choosing a variety of foods every day, you will ensure that you are supplying your body with all the essential nutrients, including vitamins and minerals, it needs. To get the balance right, it is important to know just how much of each type of food you should be eating.

There are five main food groups, and it is recommended that we should eat plenty of fruit and vegetables (at least five portions a day, not including potatoes) and foods such as cereals, pasta, rice and potatoes; moderate amounts of meat, fish, poultry and dairy products, and only small amounts of foods containing fat or sugar. By choosing a good balance of foods from these groups every day, and by choosing lower-fat or lower-sugar alternatives, we will be supplying our bodies with all the nutrients they need for optimum health.

THE FIVE MAIN FOOD GROUPS

- Fruit and vegetables
- Rice, potatoes, bread, pasta and other cereals
- Meat, poultry, fish and alternative proteins, such as peas, beans and lentils
- Milk and other dairy foods
- Foods that contain fat and foods that contain sugar

ABOVE: By choosing a variety of foods from the five main food groups, you will ensure that you are supplying your body with all the nutrients it needs.

THE ROLE AND IMPORTANCE OF FAT IN OUR DIET

Fats shouldn't be cut out of our diets completely. We need a small amount of fat for general health and well-being – fat is a valuable source of energy, and also helps to make foods more palatable to eat. However, if you lower the fats, especially saturated fats, in your diet, it may help you to lose weight as well as reducing your risk of developing some diseases, such as heart disease.

Aim to limit your daily intake of fats to no more than 30–35 per cent of the total number of calories. Since each gram of fat provides nine calories, your total daily intake should be no more than around 70g fat. Your total intake of saturated fats should be no more than approximately ten per cent of the total number of calories.

TYPES OF FAT

All fats in our foods are made up of building blocks of fatty acids and glycerol and their properties vary according to each combination.

There are two main types of fat, which are referred to as saturated and unsaturated. The unsaturated group of fats is divided into two further types – polyunsaturated and monounsaturated fats.

There is usually a combination of these types of fat (saturated, polyunsaturated and monounsaturated) in foods that contain fat, but the amount of each type varies from one kind of food to another.

SATURATED FATS

These fats are usually hard at room temperature. They are not essential in the diet, and should be limited, as they are linked to increasing the level of cholesterol in the blood, which in turn can increase the likelihood that heart disease will develop.

The main sources of saturated fats are animal products, such as fatty meats, and spreading fats, such as butter and lard, that are solid at room temperature. However, there are also saturated fats of vegetable origin, notably coconut and

BELOW: A selection of foods containing the three main types of fat: saturated, polyunsaturated and monounsaturated fats. Small quantities of poly- and monounsaturated fats can help to reduce the level of cholesterol in the blood.

palm oils, and some margarines and oils, which, when processed, change the nature of the fat from unsaturated fatty acids to saturated ones. These fats are labelled "hydrogenated vegetable oil" and should be limited. Saturated fats are also found in many processed foods, such as crisps (US potato chips) and savoury snacks, as well as cookies and cakes.

POLYUNSATURATED FATS

There are two types of polyunsaturated fats: those of vegetable or plant origin (omega 6), such as sunflower oil, soft margarine and seeds, and those from oily fish (omega 3), such as salmon, herring, mackerel and sardines. Both fats are usually liquid at room temperature. Small quantities of polyunsaturated fats are essential for good health and are thought to help reduce the blood cholesterol level.

MONOUNSATURATED FATS

Monounsaturated fats are also thought to have the beneficial effect of reducing the blood cholesterol level and this could explain why in some Mediterranean countries there is such a low incidence of heart disease. Monounsaturated fats are found in foods such as olive oil, rapeseed oil, some nuts such as almonds and hazelnuts, oily fish and avocado.

CUTTING DOWN ON FATS AND SATURATED FATS IN THE DIET

About one-quarter of the fat we eat comes from meat and meat products, one-fifth from dairy products and margarine and the rest from cakes, cookies, pastries and other foods.

It is relatively easy to cut down on obvious sources of fat in the diet, such as butter, oils, margarine, cream, full cream (whole) milk and full-fat cheese, but we also need to know about – and check our consumption of – "hidden" fats. Hidden fats can be found in foods such as cakes, crisps, cookies and nuts.

By being aware of which foods are high in fats and particularly saturated fats, and by making simple changes to your diet, you can reduce the total fat content of your diet quite considerably.

Whenever possible, choose reduced-fat or low-fat alternatives to foods such as milk, cheese and salad dressings, and fill up on very low-fat foods, such as fruit and vegetables, and foods that are high in carbohydrates, such as pasta, rice, bread and potatoes.

Cutting down on fat doesn't mean sacrificing taste. It's easy to follow a healthy-eating plan without having to forgo all your favourite foods.

EASY WAYS TO CUT DOWN ON FAT
AND SATURATED FAT IN THE DAILY DIET

There are lots of simple no-fuss ways of reducing the fat in your diet. Just follow the simple "eat less – try instead" suggestions below to discover how easy it is.

• EAT LESS – Butter, margarine, other spreading fats and cooking oils.

• TRY INSTEAD – Low-fat spread or very low-fat spread. If you must use butter or hard margarine, make sure they are softened at room temperature and spread them very thinly, or try fat-free spreads such as low-fat soft cheese for sandwiches and toast.

• EAT LESS – Fatty meats and high-fat products, such as meat pâtés, burgers, pies and sausages.

• TRY INSTEAD – Low-fat meats, such as chicken, turkey and venison. Use only the leanest cuts of meats such as lamb, beef and pork. Always cut and discard any visible fat and skin from meat before cooking. Choose reduced-fat sausages and meat products and eat fish more often. Try using low-fat protein products such as peas, beans, lentils, Quorn or tofu in place of meat in recipes.

• EAT LESS – Full-fat dairy products such as full cream (whole) milk, cream, butter,

BELOW: Chicken and fish are low in fat; always use only the leanest cuts of meats.

ABOVE: Look for reduced-fat hard cheeses, low-fat yogurts and skimmed milk.

hard margarine, crème fraîche, whole milk yogurts and hard cheese.

• TRY INSTEAD – Semi-skimmed (low-fat) or skimmed milk and milk products, low-fat yogurts, low-fat fromage frais and low-fat soft cheeses, reduced-fat hard cheeses such as Cheddar, and reduced-fat creams and crème fraîche.

• EAT LESS – Hard cooking fats, such as lard or hard margarine.

• TRY INSTEAD – Polyunsaturated or monounsaturated oils, such as olive, sunflower or corn oil for cooking (but don't use too much).

• EAT LESS – Rich salad dressings, such as full-fat mayonnaise, salad cream or French dressing.

• TRY INSTEAD – Reduced-fat or fat-free mayonnaise or dressings. Make salad dressings at home with low-fat yogurt or fromage frais.

• EAT LESS – Fried foods.

• TRY INSTEAD – Fat-free cooking methods such as grilling (broiling), microwaving, steaming or baking whenever possible. Try

cooking in a non-stick wok with only a very small amount of oil. Always roast or grill (broil) meat or poultry on a rack.

• EAT LESS – Deep-fried chips (French fries) and sautéed potatoes.

• TRY INSTEAD – Low-fat starchy foods such as pasta, couscous and rice. Choose baked or boiled potatoes, or cook oven chips occasionally.

• EAT LESS – Added fat in cooking.

• TRY INSTEAD – To cook with little or no fat. Use heavy or good quality non-stick pans so that the food doesn't stick. Try using a small amount of spray oil in cooking to control exactly how much fat you are using. Use fat-free or low-fat ingredients for cooking, such as fruit juice, low-fat or fat-free stock, wine or even beer.

• EAT LESS – High-fat snacks, such as crisps (US potato chips), tortilla chips, fried snacks and pastries, chocolate cakes, muffins, doughnuts, sweet pastries.

• TRY INSTEAD – Low-fat and fat-free fresh or dried fruits, breadsticks or vegetable sticks. Make your own home-baked low-fat cakes and bakes. Buy low-fat and reduced-fat versions of cookies.

BELOW: Rice is very low in fat and there are many varieties to choose from.

FAT-FREE COOKING METHODS

It's extremely easy to cook without fat – whenever possible, grill, bake, microwave and steam foods without the addition of fat, or try stir-frying without fat – try using a little low-fat or fat-free stock, wine or fruit juice instead.

• By choosing heavy or good quality cookware, you'll find that the amount of fat needed for cooking foods can be kept to an absolute minimum. When making casseroles or meat sauces such as Bolognese, dry fry the meat to brown it and then drain off all the excess fat before adding the other ingredients. If you do need a little fat for cooking, choose an oil that is high in unsaturates such as corn, sunflower, olive or rapeseed oil and always use as little as possible.

• When baking low-fat cakes and bakes, use good quality bakeware which doesn't need greasing before use, or use non-stick baking parchment and only lightly grease before lining.

• Look out for non-stick coated fabric sheet. This re-usable non-stick material is amazingly versatile. It can be cut to size and used to line cake tins (pans), baking sheets or frying pans. Heat-resistant up to

BELOW: Always cut and discard any visible fat and skin from meat before cooking.

ABOVE: Marinating helps to tenderize meat as well as adding flavour and colour.

290°C/550°F and microwave-safe, it will last for up to five years.

• When baking foods such as chicken or fish, rather than adding butter to the food, try baking it in a loosely sealed parcel of foil or baking parchment and adding some wine or fruit juice and herbs or spices before sealing the parcel.

• When grilling foods, the addition of fat is often unnecessary. If the food shows signs of drying, lightly brush with a small amount of unsaturated oil, such as sunflower or corn oil.

• Microwaved foods rarely need the addition of fat, so add herbs or spices for extra flavour and colour.

• Steaming or boiling are easy, fat-free ways of cooking many foods, especially vegetables, fish and chicken.

• Try poaching foods, such as chicken, fish and fruit, in low-fat or fat-free stock or syrup – it is another easy, fat-free cooking method.

• Try braising vegetables in the oven in low-fat or fat-free stock, wine or simply water with the addition of some herbs.

• Sauté vegetables in low-fat or fat-free stock, wine or fruit juice instead of oil.

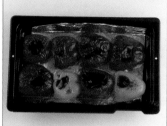

ABOVE: Vegetables can be grilled without adding any fat at all.

• Cook vegetables in a covered pan over a low heat with a little water so they cook in their own juices.

• Marinate food such as meat or poultry in mixtures of alcohol, herbs or spices, and vinegar or fruit juice. This will help to tenderize the meat and add flavour and colour. In addition, the leftover marinade can be used to baste the food occasionally while it is cooking.

• When serving vegetables such as boiled potatoes, carrots or peas, resist the temptation to add a knob of butter or margarine. Instead, sprinkle with chopped fresh herbs or ground spices.

LOW-FAT SPREADS IN COOKING

There is a huge variety of low-fat, reduced-fat and half-fat spreads available in our supermarkets, along with some spreads that are very low in fat. Generally speaking, the very low-fat spreads with a fat content of around 20 per cent or less have a high water content and so are unsuitable for cooking and only suitable for spreading.

INGREDIENTS

—

VEGETABLES

Vegetables play an important role in Italian cooking and, as many vegetables are also naturally low in fat, they are ideal for use in low-fat Italian cooking.

AUBERGINES (EGGPLANTS)

Aubergines are a popular vegetable in Italian cooking. Many different types can be found in Italian markets, the deep purple, elongated variety being the most common. Choose firm aubergines with tight, glossy skins, that feel heavy for their size.

RIGHT: Deep purple aubergines (eggplants)
BELOW: Clockwise from top left: beans, courgettes (zucchini), potatoes, tomatoes, asparagus, carrots, (bell) peppers, broccoli and mangetouts (snow peas).

COURGETTES (ZUCCHINI)

Courgettes are widely used in Italy, both as a vegetable and for their deep yellow flowers. They are available all year round but are at their best in spring and summer. The smaller and skinnier the courgettes are, the better they taste. Choose courgettes that are firm with glossy green skins and avoid those which are soft or have blemished skins. Courgettes are low in calories and fat and provide some vitamin C. They are used in many low-fat Italian dishes, and are, for example, served raw in salads, cooked with other Mediterranean vegetables such as (bell) peppers and tomatoes, or simply stuffed and oven-baked.

LEFT: Courgettes

FENNEL

Fennel has become a very popular vegetable and is used widely in low-fat Italian cooking. Bulb or Florence fennel resembles a fat white celery root and has a delicate but distinctive flavour of aniseed and a crisp, refreshing texture. Fennel is available all year round. If possible, buy it with its topknot of feathery fronds, which you can chop and use as a herb or as a garnish. Choose fennel bulbs that feel firm with crisp white outer layers that are not wizened or yellowish. It should have a delicate, fresh scent of aniseed and the texture of green celery. Whole fennel bulbs will keep in the refrigerator for up to one week. Once cut, use them immediately or the cut surfaces will discolour and soften. Fennel is naturally low in calories and fat and is enjoyed in low-fat dishes throughout Italy. It is served raw in salads, lightly dressed with a vinaigrette, or sautéed, baked or braised in similar ways to celery. It is particularly good served with white fish.

RIGHT:
Fennel

LEFT: Porcini mushrooms

MUSHROOMS

During the spring and autumn months, throughout the Italian countryside keen fungi collectors are spotted searching for the flavourful edible wild mushrooms that are a popular delicacy of Italy. Cultivated mushrooms, such as button (white) mushrooms, are rarely eaten in Italy, and Italians prefer to use dried or preserved wild fungi with their robust earthy taste. The most popular and highly prized mushroom used in Italian cooking is the porcini or cep which is also readily available dried. Other popular wild mushrooms used in Italy include field (portobello) mushrooms and chanterelles.

Cultivated mushrooms and ceps can be eaten raw (in salads or lightly dressed), but other edible wild mushrooms should be cooked before eating. In Italy, mushrooms may simply be lightly grilled (broiled) or baked or added to many dishes, such as sauces, stocks, soups and risottos.

ONIONS

Onions are an essential part of low-fat Italian cooking. Many varieties are grown, including white, mild yellow, baby (pearl) and red

LEFT: Red onion

onions. Choose firm onions that show no signs of sprouting green leaves. Onions should have thin, almost papery skins that are unblemished. Onions are naturally low in calories and fat and they are used in numerous low-fat Italian dishes. They can be served raw in salads, stuffed and baked or, in the case of baby onions, cooked in a sweet and sour sauce of sugar and wine vinegar and served cold or hot.

(BELL) PEPPERS

Generically known as capsicums, peppers come in a variety of colours including green (these are unripe red peppers), red, yellow, orange, white and purplish-black, all of which have the same sweetish flavour and crunchy texture and can be eaten raw or cooked.

ABOVE: Mixed (bell) peppers

Each region of Italy has its own low-fat specialities using peppers. These include raw or lightly cooked peppers added to salads, roasted and lightly dressed peppers, and stuffed and oven-baked peppers.

RIGHT: Vine-ripened tomatoes

TOMATOES

It is impossible to imagine low-fat Italian cooking without tomatoes. Tomatoes are cultivated all over Italy and are incorporated into the cooking of every region. In Italy, many types of tomatoes are grown, from plum to cherry tomatoes, and they are at their best in summer. Choose bright, firm, ripe tomatoes, with tight, unwrinkled, unblemished skins and a good aroma. Ripe tomatoes will keep well for several days in the refrigerator, but always bring tomatoes to room temperature before serving to enjoy them at their best.

Tomatoes are naturally low in calories and fat and provide a good source of vitamin C. Tomatoes can be enjoyed raw or cooked and they are often served with fresh basil leaves with which they have a great affinity. Tomatoes add flavour and colour to almost any savoury low-fat dish and can be enjoyed simply chopped and added to salads or made into a topping for bruschetta. They can be grilled, lightly fried, baked, stuffed or stewed and made into sauces and soups. Canned or bottled peeled plum tomatoes, passata (bottled strained tomatoes) and tomato purée or paste are also widely used in low-fat Italian cooking to add flavour, colour and texture to many dishes.

FRUIT AND NUTS

over cooked fish or lean meat to add flavour, or as an aromatic flavouring for low-fat cakes and bakes.

The Italians prefer to enjoy fruits and nuts when they are in season and much of the fresh produce available in Italy is grown or produced locally. Most types of fruit are naturally low in fat and so play a significant part in low-fat Italian cooking to create some delicious dishes.

ABOVE: Citrus fruits are an Italian favourite and can be used for both sweet and savoury recipes, melons make an excellent accompaniment to prosciutto as an antipasto, and cherries - usually preserved in syrup - are used in desserts.

FIGS

Figs are grown all over Italy and there are two main types, green and purple. Both have thin, tender skins and very sweet, succulent red flesh. Choose fruits that are soft and yielding but not squashy. Fresh figs are low in calories and fat and provide some vitamin C. Fresh figs are delicious served on their own as a typical low-fat Italian dessert, but they can also be enjoyed raw or poached in both sweet and savoury low-fat dishes.

LEFT: Purple figs

LEMONS

Lemons are grown all over Italy and their aromatic flavour enhances many low-fat Italian dishes. Depending on the variety, lemons may have a thick indented skin, or be perfectly smooth. Their appearance does not affect the flavour, but they should feel heavy for their size. Buy unwaxed lemons if you intend to use the zest in recipes. Lemons will keep in the refrigerator for up to two weeks. They are low in calories and fat and provide a good source of vitamin C. Lemons are very versatile and the juice and/or zest is added to many low-fat Italian dishes. Lemon is used in cold drinks, to add flavour to dressings and sauces, freshly squeezed

MELONS

Many different varieties of sweet aromatic melons are grown in Italy, the most common types being cantaloupe melons and watermelons. The best way to tell whether a melon is ripe is to smell it; it should have a mild, sweet scent. If it smells highly perfumed and musky it will be over-ripe. The fruit should feel heavy for its size and the skin should not be bruised or damaged. Gently press the rind with your thumbs at the stalk end; it should give a little. Melons are low in calories and fat and provide some vitamin C. Typically, Italians enjoy melon as a low-fat appetizer, simply served on its own or with wafer-thin slices of prosciutto, or as a tasty dessert served on its own or in a fresh fruit salad, sorbet or granita.

BELOW: Watermelon

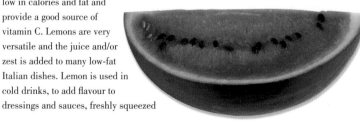

ABOVE: The Italian climate is perfect for growing oranges; they add a bright splash of colour to salads and desserts.

ORANGES

Many varieties of oranges are grown in Sicily and southern Italy, the best-known Sicilian oranges being the small blood oranges with their bright ruby-red flesh. Other types include sweet navel and bitter oranges. Choose unwaxed oranges if you intend to use the zest in recipes. Oranges are naturally low in calories and fat and provide a good source of vitamin C. Oranges are served in both sweet and savoury low-fat dishes across Italy, including in salads, desserts, sorbets or granitas.

PEACHES AND NECTARINES

Peaches and nectarines with their sweet juicy flesh are summer fruits grown in Italy. Both fruits are available in either yellow or

ABOVE: Peaches

white fleshed varieties, all of which are succulent, juicy and full of flavour. They are naturally low in calories and fat and provide some vitamin C. Peaches and nectarines are interchangeable in recipes and are delicious served as a dessert fruit but can also be macerated in fortified wine or spirits or poached in white wine or syrup to create a typical low-fat Italian dessert. They are also delicious served with raspberries or made into fruit drinks, low-fat ice creams and sorbets.

ALMONDS AND OTHER NUTS

Two varieties of almonds are grown in Italy – sweet and bitter almonds. Sweet almonds are the most common and are eaten on their own or used in cooking and baking. Bitter almonds are not edible in their raw state and are used to flavour liqueurs such as amaretto. In Italy, sweet almonds are enjoyed raw as a dessert or dried and blanched, flaked (sliced) or ground for use in cakes, bakes and confectionery. Dried sweet almonds are the most common type used in many countries. Almonds are high in mono-unsaturated fat and low in saturated fat.

Other nuts, such as hazelnuts, walnuts and pistachios, are also grown and harvested in Italy and are used in many sweet and savoury dishes, including desserts, confections, cakes and bakes. Hazelnuts are usually dried before use, whereas walnuts can be enjoyed fresh or dried and pistachios are eaten raw or roasted. As with many nuts, they are all high in fat, although the type of fats they

LEFT: Pine nuts (top) and almonds (below)

contain are the "healthier" types – either monounsaturated or poly-unsaturated fats. They are all low in saturated fat but should be used sparingly in low-fat cooking.

PINE NUTS

Pine nuts or pine kernels are very popular in Italy and are an essential ingredient in the classic Italian pesto sauce. They can be eaten either raw or toasted and are used in both sweet and savoury dishes. Pine nuts are high in polyunsaturated fat and low in saturated fat and they should be used in moderation.

BELOW: Almonds are an extremely versatile ingredient, used raw or to flavour cakes and liqueurs. Red and white Italian grapes are particularly refreshing on a hot day; they have a wonderful Muscat flavour.

PASTA

Pasta is the one ingredient that probably sums up the essence of Italian cooking, and it is an essential part of many Italian meals. It is a wonderfully simple, nutritious and low-fat food which is available in a whole wealth of shapes and sizes. There are two basic types of pasta, dried and fresh.

FRESH PASTA

Home-made fresh pasta is usually made by hand using superfine plain (all-purpose) white flour enriched with eggs. It is often wrapped around a low-fat stuffing of lean meat, fish, vegetables or low-fat cheese to make filled pasta such as ravioli or tortellini, or layered with lean meat or vegetable sauces to make a tasty low-fat lasagne. Commercially-made fresh pasta is made with durum wheat, water and eggs. The flavour and texture of all fresh pasta is very delicate, so it is best suited to slightly more creamy, low-fat sauces.

DRIED PASTA

Dried pasta is produced from a dough made from hard durum wheat. It is then shaped into numerous different forms, from long, thin spaghetti to elaborate spirals and frilly bow shapes. Dried pasta can be made from basic pasta dough, which consists of durum wheat and water, or it can be made from a dough enriched with eggs or coloured and flavoured with ingredients such as

LEFT: Dried rigatoni

ABOVE: Fresh pasta comes in a wide variety of interesting shapes, sizes and colours.

LEFT: Angel's hair pasta

RIGHT: Fettucine

spinach, herbs, tomatoes or squid ink. Dried pasta has a nutty flavour and should always retain a firm texture when cooked. It is generally used in preference to fresh pasta for thinner-textured, more robust, low-fat sauces.

BUYING AND STORING PASTA

Choose dried pasta that is made from Italian durum wheat and store it in a cool, dry place. Once opened, dried pasta will keep for weeks in an airtight container. Home-made fresh pasta will only keep for a couple of days, but it also freezes very well. Commercially made fresh pasta (fresh pasta that is available in a chilled compartment in the supermarket) is

RIGHT: Dried spaghetti

pasteurized and vacuum-packed, so it will keep in the refrigerator for about two weeks, or it can be frozen for up to six months. When buying coloured and flavoured pasta, make sure that it has been made with natural ingredients.

COOKING PASTA

All pasta must be cooked in a large pan filled with plenty of fast-boiling, salted water. Cooking times vary according to the type, size and shape of the pasta but, as a general rule, filled pasta takes about 12 minutes, dried pasta needs 8–10 minutes and fresh pasta only 2–3 minutes. All pasta should be cooked until it is al dente, or still firm to the bite. Always test pasta for readiness just before you think it should be done as it can easily overcook. To stop it cooking, take the pan off the heat and run a little cold water into it, then drain the pasta and serve.

PASTA VARIETIES

Pasta shapes can be divided roughly into four categories: long strands or ribbons, flat, short and filled. When choosing the appropriate pasta for a sauce, there are no hard-and-fast rules; almost any pasta is suitable for a low-fat sauce.

LEFT: Conchiglie

BELOW: Tomato and spinach orecchiette

SHORT PASTA

Short pasta covers a wide variety of shapes, the more common types being macaroni, rigati, rigatoni and tubetti. Pasta shapes vary and the list is almost endless, with some wonderfully descriptive names. There are cappellacci (little hats), orecchiette (little ears) or maltagliati (badly cut) and penne (quills), conchiglie (little shells), farfalle (bows) and lumache (snails).

LONG OR RIBBON PASTA

The best-known long variety is spaghetti, which also comes in a thinner version, spaghettini, and the flatter linguine, which means "little tongues". Bucatini are thicker and hollow – perfect for trapping low-fat sauces in the cavity. Ribbon pasta is wider than the strands and fettucine, tagliatelle and trenette all fall into this category. Dried tagliatelle is usually sold folded into nests, which unravel during cooking. Pappardelle are the widest ribbon pasta; they are often served with a low-fat rabbit sauce. The thinnest pasta strands are vermicelli (little worms) and ultra-fine capelli d'angelo (angel's hair).

FLAT PASTA

In Italy, fresh flat pasta is often called maccheroni, not to be confused with the short tubes of macaroni with which we are familiar. Lasagne and cannelloni are larger flat rectangles of pasta, used for layering or rolling round a low-fat filling; dried cannelloni are already formed into wide tubes. Layered pasta dishes like this are cooked in the oven.

RIGHT: Lasagne

BELOW: Multi-coloured tagliatelle

RIGHT: Tortelli

FILLED PASTA

Dried and fresh filled pastas are available in many varieties and there are dozens of names for filled pasta, but the only difference lies in the shape and size. Ravioli are square, tortelli and agnolotti are usually round, while tortellini and anellini are ring-shaped. Fillings for fresh and dried pasta include lean meat, pumpkin, artichokes, ricotta and spinach, seafood, chicken and mushrooms.

GNOCCHI

Gnocchi fall into a different category from other pasta, being similar to small dumplings. They can be made from semolina (milled durum wheat), flour, potatoes or ricotta and spinach and may be shaped like elongated shells, ovals, cylinders or flat discs, or roughly shredded into strozzapreti (priest stranglers). Gnocchi are extremely light and almost melt in the mouth and can be served like any pasta, as a low-fat first course, in clear soup or as an accompaniment to the main course.

RIGHT: Gnocchi

BREAD, RICE, GRAINS, BEANS, PEAS AND LEINTILS

ABOVE: Ciabatta

Rice, grains, beans, peas and lentils form the basis of many delicious and nutritious low-fat Italian dishes and fresh bread is always served in Italy as a tasty, low-fat accompaniment to every meal.

In Italy, no meal is ever served without bread. There are numerous different types of Italian breads with many regional variations. Several varieties, such as ciabatta and focaccia are readily available from bakers or supermarkets.

Rice and grains are staple foods in Italy and are almost as important as pasta in Italian cooking. Italy relied heavily on these low-fat, protein-rich foods when luxuries such as meat were in short supply, and a whole host of wholesome and delicious low fat recipes were developed using these modest ingredients.

Many beans, peas and lentils, both fresh and dried, are naturally low in fat and are used widely in low-fat Italian cooking, providing the basis for a variety of delicious dishes.

CIABATTA

These flattish, slipper-shaped loaves with squared or rounded ends are made with olive oil and are often flavoured with fresh or dried herbs, olives or sun-dried tomatoes. They have an airy texture inside and a pale, crisp crust. Ciabatta is delicious served warm and is excellent for low-fat sandwiches.

FOCACCIA

Focaccia is a dimpled flat bread similar to pizza dough which is traditionally lightly oiled and baked in a wood oven. A whole traditional focaccia from an Italian bakery weighs several kilos and is sold by weight, cut into manageable pieces. A variety of low-fat ingredients can be worked into the dough or served as a topping – onions, rosemary or oregano, lean ham or olives.

LEFT: Focaccia

RIGHT: Risotto rices like these arborio varieties are famous in Italy, and can be flavoured with an almost endless array of ingredients.

RICE

Italy produces a great variety of rice including the short-grain carnaroli and arborio rice, which make the best risottos. Italian rice is classified by size, ranging from the shortest, roundest ordinario (used for puddings), to semifino (for soups and salads), then fino and finally the longer grains of the finest risotto rice, superfino.

Rice is used in many low-fat Italian dishes. Baked rice dishes are also popular or plain boiled rice may simply be served on its own.

The most famous of all Italian rice dishes, however, is risotto. A good risotto can be made only with superfine rice and provides a delicious low-fat Italian meal. All risottos are basically prepared in the same way, although they can be flavoured with an almost endless variety of exciting ingredients.

Buy only superfine risotto rice for use in Italian risottos. Shorter grain rice is best reserved for making soups and puddings. Store uncooked rice in an airtight container in a cool, dry place. The rice will keep for several months.

ABOVE: Fine polenta

POLENTA

For centuries, polenta has been a staple low-fat food of northern Italy. Polenta is a grainy yellow flour which is a type of cornmeal made from ground maize. It is then cooked into a kind of porridge and used in a variety of ways. There are two main types of polenta – coarse and fine.

Polenta is very versatile and can be used to create many delicious low-fat dishes. It is most often served in Italy as a first course but it can also be used as a

ABOVE: Canned borlotti beans

LEFT: Canned black-eyed beans (peas)

vegetable dish or main course. Plain boiled polenta can be served on its own to make a satisfying dish. It goes well with lean meats and game or it can be cooled and cut into squares before being grilled (broiled) or baked and served with a low-fat sauce or topping.

Quick-cooking polenta, which can be prepared in only five minutes, and ready-prepared blocks of cooked polenta are also available, but traditional polenta only takes about 20 minutes to cook, so it is best to buy this for its superior texture and flavour. Once opened, polenta will keep in an airtight container for at least one month.

HARICOT (NAVY) BEANS

Haricot beans are eaten all over Italy, the most popular varieties being borlotti beans, cannellini beans (a type of kidney bean) and black-eyed beans (peas). All these are eaten in hearty low-fat stews, with pasta, in low-fat soups or salads or simply cooked and served as a side dish.

Both fresh and dried beans are available in Italy and canned varieties make an acceptable substitute. Once opened, store dried beans in an airtight container in a cool, dry place for up to one year.

BROAD (FAVA) BEANS

Broad beans are at their best when eaten fresh from the pod in late spring or early summer when they are small and very tender, or cooked and skinned later in the season. They are popular in Italy and are

LEFT: Canned broad (fava) beans

excellent served with lean ham, in other low-fat dishes such as risotto or simply served as a vegetable accompaniment. Dried broad beans, which need pre-cooking, are also used in Italian dishes such as low-fat soups and stews.

CHICKPEAS

Chickpeas, which are round, golden pulses shaped rather like hazelnuts, and which have a distinctive, nutty flavour, are also popular in low-fat Italian cooking. chickpeas are cooked and used in the same way as haricot beans and they can also be served cold and lightly dressed to make a tasty salad.

LENTILS

Lentils grow in pods although they are always sold podded and dried. Italian lentils are the small brown variety which do not break up during cooking and are often mixed with pasta or rice to create delicious and satisfying low-fat dishes. They are also delicious served cold, lightly dressed or in nutritious soups. Whole brown, green or puy lentils can also be used.

ABOVE: Dried chickpeas

RIGHT: Dried brown lentils

DAIRY PRODUCTS

Dairy products such as butter and cheeses play a part in low-fat Italian cooking but due to their generally high fat content they should only be used in small amounts.

LEFT: Butter

RIGHT: Mozzarella

BUTTER
Although olive oil is the primary fat used for cooking in Italy, butter is used more commonly in northern Italian cooking. The quantity of butter used in recipes in this book has been kept to a minimum as butter is very high in fat, particularly saturated fat. Choose a polyunsaturated or mono-unsaturated margarine in place of butter if you prefer. Although the fat content of these margarines is similar to butter, the fats are "healthier" types. Very low-fat spreads are not suitable for cooking; only use these for spreading.

CHEESES
Italy has a great variety of cheese, ranging from fresh, mild cheese such as mozzarella to mature (sharp) hard cheeses such as Parmesan. All types of milk are used, including cow's, ewe's, goat's and buffalo's and some cheeses are made from a mixture of milks. Other popular types of Italian cheese include Pecorino, Provolone, Bel Paese, Fontina, ricotta, Gorgonzola and mascarpone.

Many of the Italian cheeses are suitable for cooking and are used in a wide variety of dishes. However, many are also high in fat, especially saturated fat, but if used in moderation can be incorporated into low-fat Italian cuisine. Strong-flavoured cheeses, such as Parmesan, can be used in smaller quantities and other cheeses, such as mozzarella, are available in reduced-fat versions.

ABOVE: Parmesan

PARMESAN
Parmesan is the best-known and most important of the Italian hard cheeses. There are two basic types – Parmigiano Reggiano and Grana Padano – but the former is infinitely superior. A little finely grated Parmesan adds delicious flavour to many dishes from pasta and polenta to risotto and minestrone.

LEFT: Pecorino studded with peppercorns

RIGHT: Ricotta

MOZZARELLA
Italian cooking could hardly exist without mozzarella, the pure white egg-shaped fresh cheese, whose melting quality makes it perfect for so many dishes. The best mozzarella is made in the area around Naples, using water buffalo's milk. Reduced-fat mozzarella is also readily available and is ideal for use in low-fat Italian cooking. It is delicious in sandwiches or served with fresh red tomatoes and green basil (*insalata tricolore*, or three-colour salad). When cooked, mozzarella becomes uniquely stringy and is ideal for topping pizzas.

RICOTTA
Ricotta is a fresh, soft cheese made from cow's, ewe's or goat's milk. It is used widely in Italy for both sweet and savoury recipes. Ricotta has a medium fat content so should be used in moderation in low-fat Italian cooking. It has an excellent texture and a mild flavour, so it makes a perfect vehicle for seasonings such as black pepper, nutmeg or chopped fresh herbs. It is also puréed with cooked spinach to make a classic filling for ravioli, cannelloni or lasagne. It is often used in desserts and it can be sweetened and then served with fresh fruit.

OLIVE OIL AND FLAVOURINGS

Olive oil and flavourings play an important role in Italian cooking. They are ideal for combining with staples such as rice and pasta to create speedy and nutritious low-fat meals.

OLIVE OIL

Olive oil is perhaps the single most important ingredient in an Italian kitchen. The best olive oil is extra virgin, which must have an acidity level of less than one per cent. It is ideal for using "raw" in salad dressings, uncooked sauces and for drizzling lightly over vegetables. Virgin olive oil has a higher acidity level and less refined flavour and is used as a condiment or for general cooking. Unclassified or pure olive oil is refined, then blended with virgin oil to add flavour and is ideal for cooking and baking.

Olive oil is high in monounsaturated fat and low in saturated fat and should be used in moderation when preparing low-fat Italian recipes.

ABOVE: Italian flavourings are essential for the store cupboard; a variety of oils, sun-dried tomatoes and tomato purée (paste), passata (bottled strained tomatoes), anchovies, capers and balsamic vinegar.

RIGHT: A mixture of black and green olives

BALSAMIC VINEGAR

Balsamic vinegar is the king of vinegars and is made in the area around Modena in Italy. It is the boiled and concentrated juice of local trebbiano grapes, which is aged over a very long period to give it a slightly syrupy texture and a rich, deep mahogany colour. Balsamic vinegar is used as a dressing or to finish a delicate sauce for white fish, poultry or calf's liver.

OLIVES

Black and green olives are used in low-fat Italian cooking, and both types are available whole or pitted, sold loose, in jars or vacuum-packed. Olives are added to many low-fat Italian dishes, such as salads and sauces. Olives are quite high in monounsaturated fat and low in saturated fat, but should be used in moderation.

PESTO

Green pesto is traditionally made with fresh basil, pine nuts, Parmesan and olive oil, but a red version based on sweet red (bell) peppers is also available. It can be home-made or bought ready-made in jars or fresh in tubs. Pesto can be added to hot pasta or gnocchi, risottos, tomato sauces or tomato-based soups. However, pesto is high in fat and should be used sparingly.

SUN-DRIED TOMATOES

Wrinkled red sun-dried tomatoes are available dry in packets or preserved in oil in jars. Dry-packed tomatoes are lower in fat than the oil-packed ones and are used in many low-fat Italian dishes to add flavour and colour. They can be eaten on their own as a snack, or soaked in hot water until soft, then added to numerous dishes including low-fat sauces, soups, egg and vegetable dishes.

RIGHT: Sun-dried tomatoes

LEFT: Extra virgin olive oil

BELOW: Balsamic vinegar

THE CALORIE CONTENTS OF FOOD

When calorie counting it is important to account for everything you eat, including accompaniments and healthy snacks, as well as drinks. Here is a list of the calorie counts for some common foods, but you should also check the packet as counts can vary from brand to brand and according to size:

FOOD TYPE	PORTION/QUANTITY	KCAL
Long-grain white rice (uncooked)	50g/2oz/¼ cup	198Kcal
Long-grain brown rice (uncooked)	50g/2oz/¼ cup	182Kcal
Boiled new potatoes	150g/6oz	105Kcal
Boiled old potatoes	150g/6oz	136Kcal
Baked potato	115g/4oz	156Kcal
White pasta (raw weight)	50g/2oz/½ cup	188Kcal
Wholemeal (whole-wheat) pasta (uncooked)	50g/2oz/½ cup	158Kcal
Zero-calorie pasta	50g/2oz/½ cup	2Kcal
Cooked egg noodles	50g/2oz/½ cup	215Kcal
Zero-calorie noodles	50g/2oz/½ cup	2Kcal
Medium-sliced white bread	1 slice/36g/1½oz	78Kcal
Medium-sliced wholemeal bread	1 slice/36g/1½oz	85Kcal
Toast with butter and jam	1 slice/36g/1½oz	125Kcal
Flatbread	x1/85g/3oz	90Kcal
White pitta bread	x1/85g/3oz	124Kcal
Wholemeal pitta bread	x1/85g/3oz	146Kcal
Plain breadstick	1	20Kcal
Plain thin rice cake	1	19Kcal
Carrot sticks	50g/2oz	18Kcal
(Bell) pepper strips	50g/2oz	14Kcal
Celery sticks	50g/2oz	5Kcal
Cooked broccoli	50g/2oz	18Kcal
Cooked carrots	50g/2oz	17Kcal

Cooked greens (collards)	50g/2oz	14Kcal
Green leafy salad	50g/2oz	8Kcal
Low-fat natural (plain) yogurt	115g/4oz/½ cup	65Kcal
Banana	1 medium fruit	105Kcal
Apple	1 medium fruit	51Kcal
Orange	1 medium fruit	62Kcal
Strawberries, raw, fresh	115g/4oz/⅔ cup	32Kcal
Blueberries, raw, fresh	115g/4oz/1 cup	62Kcal
Raisins	25g/1oz/⅕ cup	68Kcal
Dried apricots	25g/1oz/⅛ cup	47Kcal
Mixed nuts, unsalted	25g/1oz/¼ cup	170Kcal
Mixed seeds	25g/1oz/⅕ cup	150Kcal
Muesli (granola) with semi-skimmed (low-fat) milk	50g/2oz/½ cup	216Kcal
Bran flakes with semi-skimmed milk	30g/generous 1oz/1⅓ cups	157Kcal
Fresh orange juice	250ml/8fl oz/1 cup	108Kcal
Black coffee	250ml/8fl oz/1 cup	10Kcal
White coffee with semi-skimmed milk	250ml/8fl oz/1 cup	20Kcal
Latte, regular	250ml/8fl oz/1 cup	136Kcal
Cappuccino, full-cream (whole) milk	250ml/8fl oz/1 cup	125Kcal
Tea with semi-skimmed milk	250ml/8fl oz/1 cup	15Kcal
Red wine	120ml/4fl oz/½ cup	85Kcal
White wine	120ml/4fl oz/½ cup	90Kcal
Lager	300ml/10fl oz/1¼ cups	160Kcal

EQUIPMENT

Many of the utensils in the Italian kitchen are everyday items found in most kitchens, but some specialized ones are particularly useful.

For pasta you need to have a large pan for cooking the pasta and a colander for draining, while for making sauces you need only a sharp knife and a cutting board for chopping ingredients and a pan for cooking. You will also need a large bowl plus spoons and forks for tossing and serving.

You can make pasta by hand, but a pasta machine will make it much lighter work. Pasta machines come in electric or hand-cranked varieties.

BELOW: If you make pasta frequently, a pasta machine is an excellent buy because it is inexpensive, easy and fun to use, and makes excellent pasta in a very short time.

A special spoon with "teeth" or a perforated ladle are ideal for lifting spaghetti out of the pan. If you are making pizza, a cutting wheel will cut it into clean slices.

To keep fat to an absolute minimum, choose heavy, good quality cookware which doesn't need greasing before use, or use baking parchment and only lightly grease the tin (pan) before lining it. Also look out for non-stick coated fabric sheet, which is reusable.

BISCUIT (COOKIE) CUTTER
Usually used for cutting biscuit dough into fancy shapes but is equally good for cutting fresh pasta shapes.

COLANDER
Indispensable for draining hot pasta and cooked vegetables.

EARTHENWARE POT
Excellent for slow-cooking stews, soups or sauces. It can be used either in the oven or on top of the stove on a gentle heat with a metal heat diffuser under it to prevent cracking. Many shapes and sizes are available. To season a terracotta pot before using it for the first time, immerse it in cold water overnight. Remove from the water and rub the unglazed bottom with a garlic clove. Fill with water and bring slowly to the boil. Discard the water. Repeat, changing the water, until the "earth" taste disappears.

FLUTED PASTRY CUTTER
Good for cutting out fresh pasta shapes or for cutting freshly rolled pastry.

HAND FOOD MILL
Excellent for soups, sauces and tomato "passata": the pulp passes through the holes of the mill, leaving the seeds and skin behind.

ICE CREAM SCOOP
Suited to scooping firm and well-frozen ice creams, sorbets and yogurt ices.

ITALIAN ICE CREAM SCOOP
Good for soft ices or sorbets that are not too solid.

MEAT HAMMER
Good for pounding escalopes. As well as pounding meat, it can be used to crush nuts and whole spices.

MORTAR AND PESTLE
Useful for hand-grinding spices, rock salt, whole peppercorns, fresh or dried herbs and breadcrumbs.

ABOVE: 1 Earthenware pot, 2 olive stoner, 3 whisk, 4 fluted pastry cutter, 5 biscuit cutters, 6 pasta rolling pin, 7 mortar and pestle, 8 hand food mill, 9 colander, 10 Parmesan cheese knife, 11 pizza cutting wheel, 12 palette knife, 13 spaghetti spoon, 14 meat hammer, 15 pasta machine, 16 wide vegetable peeler, 17 Italian ice cream scoop, 18 ice cream scoop.

OLIVE STONER (PITTER)
Can be used for stoning black or green olives or fresh cherries.

PALETTE KNIFE
Very useful for spreading and smoothing.

PARMESAN CHEESE KNIFE
Break Parmesan off the large cheese wheels using this wedge-shaped tool.

PASTA MACHINE
Many models are available, including sophisticated electric and industrial models. Most have an adjustable roller width and both thin and wide noodle cutters.

PASTA ROLLING PIN
Ideal for rolling out home-made pasta dough. A length of dowelling 5cm/2in in diameter can also be used. Smooth the surface with fine sandpaper before using for the first time.

PIZZA CUTTING WHEEL
Useful for cutting slices of pizza, although a sharp knife may also be used.

SPAGHETTI SPOON
The wooden "teeth" catch the spaghetti strands and make cooked spaghetti easier to serve.

WHISK
Excellent for smoothing sauces and beating egg whites.

WIDE VEGETABLE PEELER
Very effective and easy to use for peeling all sizes of vegetable. Can also be used for peeling fruit.

MAKING BASIC PASTA DOUGH ON A WORK SURFACE

The best place to make, knead and roll out pasta dough is on a wooden kitchen table – the larger the better. The surface should be warm, so marble is not suitable.

INGREDIENTS

200g/7oz/1¾ cups plain (all-purpose) flour
pinch of salt
2 eggs
10ml/2 tsp cold water

SERVES 3–4

VARIATIONS

TOMATO: add 20ml/4 tsp tomato purée (paste) to the eggs before mixing.
SPINACH: add 115g/4oz frozen spinach, thawed and squeezed of excess moisture. Liquidize with the eggs, before adding to the flour.
HERB: add 45ml/3 tbsp finely chopped fresh herbs to the eggs before mixing the dough.

1 Sift the flour and salt on to a clean work surface and make a well in the centre with your hand.

2 Put the eggs and water into the well. Using a fork, beat the eggs gently together, then gradually draw in the flour from the sides, to make a thick paste.

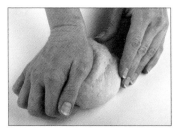

3 When the mixture becomes too stiff to use a fork, use your hands to mix to a firm dough. Knead the dough for about 5 minutes, until smooth. (This can be done in an electric food mixer fitted with a dough hook.) Wrap in clear film (plastic wrap) to prevent it drying out and leave to rest for 20–30 minutes.

MAKING BASIC PASTA DOUGH IN A BOWL

1 Sift the flour and salt into a glass bowl and make a well in the centre. Add the eggs and water.

2 Using a fork, beat the eggs gently together, then gradually draw in the flour from the sides, to make a thick paste.

3 When the mixture becomes too stiff to use a fork, use your hands to mix to a firm dough. Knead the dough for 5 minutes until smooth. (This can be done in an electric food mixer fitted with a dough hook.) Wrap in clear film to prevent it drying out and leave for 20–30 minutes.

ROLLING OUT PASTA DOUGH BY HAND

 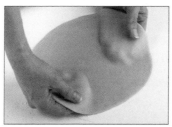 

1 Cut the basic dough in quarters. Use one quarter at a time and re-wrap the rest in clear film so it does not dry out. Flatten the dough and dust liberally with flour. Start rolling out the dough, making sure you roll it evenly.

2 As the dough becomes thinner, keep on rotating it on the work surface by gently lifting the edges with your fingers and supporting it over the rolling pin. Make sure you don't tear the dough.

3 Carry on rolling out the dough until it has reached the desired thickness, about 3mm/¹/₈in thick.

ROLLING OUT DOUGH USING A PASTA MACHINE

1 Cut the basic dough into quarters. Use one quarter at a time and re-wrap the rest in clear film so it does not dry out. Flatten the dough and dust liberally with flour. Start with the machine set to roll at the thickest setting. Pass the dough through the rollers several times, dusting the dough from time to time with flour until it is smooth.

2 Fold the strip of dough into three, press the joins well together and pass through the machine again. Repeat the folding and rolling several times on each setting.

3 Guide the dough through the machine but do not pull or stretch it or the dough will tear. As the dough is worked through all the settings, it will become thinner and longer. Guide the dough over your hand, as the dough is rolled out to a thin sheet. Pasta used for stuffing, such as ravioli or tortellini, should be used straightaway. Otherwise lay the rolled sheets on a clean dish towel, lightly dusted with sifted flour, and leave to dry for 10 minutes before cutting. This makes it easier to cut and prevents the strands of pasta sticking together.

CUTTING PASTA SHAPES

Until you are confident at handling and shaping pasta dough, it is easier to work with small
quantities. Always keep the dough well wrapped in clear film (plastic wrap) to prevent it drying
out, before you are ready to work with it.

CUTTING OUT TAGLIATELLE
To cut tagliatelle, fit the appropriate
attachment to the machine or move the
handle to the appropriate slot. Cut the
pasta sheets into 25cm/10in lengths
and pass these through the machine as
for spaghetti.

CUTTING OUT LASAGNE
Take a sheet of pasta dough and cut out
neat rectangles about 18 × 7.5cm/7 × 3in
to make sheets of lasagne. Lay on a clean
dish towel to dry.

CUTTING OUT SPAGHETTI
To cut spaghetti, fit the appropriate
attachment to the machine or move the
handle to the appropriate slot. Cut the
pasta sheets into 25cm/10in lengths and
pass these through the machine. Guide
the strands over the back of your hand as
they appear out of the machine.

SHAPING RAVIOLI

Ravioli made in this way are not perfectly square, but they look charmingly home-made.

1 To make ravioli, place spoonfuls of
filling on a sheet of dough at intervals of
5–7.5cm/2–3in, leaving a 2.5cm/1in
border. Brush the dough between the
spoonfuls of filling with lightly beaten
egg white.

2 Lay a second sheet of pasta carefully
over the top. Press around each mound of
filling, excluding any air pockets.

3 Using a fluted pastry wheel or a sharp
knife, cut between the stuffing to make
square-shaped parcels.

MAKING FARFALLE (PASTA BOWS)

1 Roll the pasta dough through a pasta machine until the sheets are very thin. Then cut into long strips 4cm/1½in wide.

2 Cut the strips into small rectangles. Run a pastry wheel along the two shorter edges of the little rectangles – this will give the bows a decorative edge.

3 Moisten the centre of the strips and using a finger and thumb, gently pinch each rectangle together in the middle to make little pasta bows.

MAKING TAGLIATELLE

1 Lightly flour some spinach-flavoured pasta dough, cut into a rectangle 30 × 10cm/12 × 4in and roll it up.

2 Using a sharp knife, cut straight across the pasta roll.

3 Carefully unravel each little roll as you cut it to make ribbons of fresh tagliatelle.

COOKING PASTA

1 Before starting to cook either sauce or pasta, read through the recipe carefully. It is important to know which needs to be cooked for the longest time – sometimes it is the pasta and sometimes the sauce, so don't always assume one or the other. The sauce can often be made ahead of time and reheated, but pasta is almost like a hot soufflé – it waits for no one.

2 There needs to be plenty of room for the pasta to move around in the large amount of water it requires, so a big pan is essential. The best type of pan is a tall, lightweight, straight-sided, stainless steel pasta cooking pot with its own in-built draining pan. Both outer and inner pans have two handles each, which ensures easy and safe lifting and draining. It is well worth investing in one of these pans.

3 Use a large quantity of water. If there is not enough water, the pasta shapes will stick together as they swell and the pan will become overcrowded. This will result in gummy-textured pasta. Before adding the pasta, the water should be at a fast rolling boil. The quickest way to do this is to boil water in the kettle, then pour it into the pasta pan, which should be set over high heat.

SOUPS

DELICIOUS *soups can be made in no time*
at all and they provide a TEMPTING *start*
to a meal or make a complete LIGHT *meal*
on their own when served with a hunk of fresh
crusty ITALIAN *bread. We include a*
selection of home-made LOW-FAT *Italian*
soups for you to make and enjoy such as
Roasted PEPPER *Soup, Italian Vegetable*
Soup, Chicken and Pasta Soup and Roasted
TOMATO *and Pasta Soup.*

LITTLE STUFFED HATS IN BROTH

—

This soup is served in northern Italy on Santo Stefano (St Stephen's Day – or Boxing Day)
and on New Year's Day. It makes a light change from all the celebration food the day before.

INGREDIENTS
1.2 litres/2 pints/5 cups chicken stock
90–115g/3¹/2–4oz/1 cup fresh or
dried cappelletti
30ml/2 tbsp dry white wine (optional)
about 15ml/1 tbsp finely chopped fresh flat
leaf parsley (optional)
salt and ground black pepper
shredded flat leaf parsley, to garnish
15ml/1 tbsp grated fresh Parmesan cheese,
to serve

SERVES 4

1 Pour the chicken stock into a large pan
and bring to the boil. Add a little salt and
pepper to taste.

2 Drop in the pasta, stir well and bring
back to the boil. Reduce the heat to a
simmer and cook, according to the
packet instructions, until the pasta
is tender or al dente. Stir the pasta
frequently during cooking to ensure that
it cooks evenly.

3 Swirl in the wine and parsley, if using,
then adjust the seasoning. Ladle into
warmed soup bowls, then sprinkle with
shredded flat leaf parsley and grated
Parmesan. Serve immediately.

NUTRITIONAL NOTES
Per portion:

Energy	103Kcals/436kJ
Total fat	1.7g
Saturated fat	0.8g
Cholesterol	3.7mg
Fibre	0.8g

TINY PASTA IN BROTH

—

In Italy this tasty pasta soup is often served with bread for a light evening supper or for a quick
midday snack. You can use any other dried tiny soup pastas in place of the funghetti.

INGREDIENTS
1.2 litres/2 pints/5 cups beef stock
75g/3oz/³/4 cup dried tiny soup pasta,
such as funghetti
2 pieces bottled roasted red (bell) pepper,
about 50g/2oz
salt and ground black pepper
25g/1oz coarsely shaved fresh Parmesan
cheese, to serve

SERVES 4

1 Bring the beef stock to the boil in a
large pan. Add salt and pepper to taste,
then drop in the dried soup pasta. Stir
well and bring the stock back to the boil.

2 Reduce the heat to a simmer and cook
for 7–8 minutes, or according to the
packet instructions, until the pasta is
tender or al dente. Stir frequently during
cooking to prevent the pasta shapes from
sticking together.

NUTRITIONAL NOTES
Per portion:

Energy	108Kcals/457kJ
Total fat	3.7g
Saturated fat	1.5g
Cholesterol	6.2mg
Fibre	0.8g

3 Drain the pieces of roasted pepper and
dice them finely. Place them in the
bottom of four soup bowls. Taste the soup
and adjust the seasoning. Ladle into
soup bowls and serve immediately, with
shavings of Parmesan served separately.

ROASTED PEPPER SOUP

—

Grilling intensifies the flavour of red and yellow peppers and helps this soup keep its stunning
colour. No added fat is used for this recipe, creating a delicious and virtually fat-free soup.

INGREDIENTS

3 red (bell) peppers
1 yellow (bell) pepper
1 onion, chopped
1 garlic clove, crushed
750ml/1¼ pints/3 cups vegetable stock
15ml/1 tbsp plain (all-purpose) flour
salt and ground black pepper
diced (bell) peppers, to garnish

SERVES 4

1 Preheat the grill (broiler). Halve the
red and yellow peppers and cut out and
discard their stalks and white pith.
Scrape out and discard the seeds.

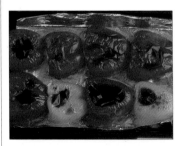

2 Line a grill (broiling) pan with foil and
arrange the halved peppers, skin-side up,
in a single layer. Grill (broil) under a
hot grill until the skins have blackened
and blistered.

3 Transfer the grilled (broiled) peppers to
a plastic bag and leave for a few minutes.
Once cool, gently peel away and discard
their skins. Roughly chop the pepper
flesh. Set aside.

4 Put the onion, garlic clove and
150ml/¼ pint/⅔ cup stock into a large
pan. Bring to the boil and boil for about
5 minutes until most of the stock has
reduced in volume. Reduce the heat and
stir until the onion and garlic are softened
and just beginning to colour.

NUTRITIONAL NOTES

Per portion:

Energy	28Kcals/117kJ
Total fat	0.2g
Saturated fat	0.04g
Cholesterol	0mg
Fibre	0.8g

5 Sprinkle the flour over the onions, then
gradually stir in the remaining stock. Add
the chopped peppers and bring to the
boil, stirring. Cover and allow to simmer
for 5 minutes.

6 Leave to cool slightly, then purée in a
blender or food processor until smooth.
Season to taste. Return to the rinsed-out
pan and reheat until piping hot. Ladle
into soup bowls and garnish each portion
with a sprinkling of diced peppers. Serve.

COOK'S TIP

Sautéeing onions and garlic in stock,
as described in Step 4, is a very useful
technique in low-fat cooking. The trick
is to allow the stock to reduce almost
entirely, from which point the onions
and garlic will start to brown, rather
than simply being boiled.

PASTA AND CHICKPEA SOUP

A simple, country-style Italian soup, ideal for a flavourful, low-fat appetizer. You can use other
pasta shapes, but conchiglie are ideal because they scoop up the chickpeas and beans.

INGREDIENTS

1 onion
2 carrots
2 celery sticks
15ml/1 tbsp olive oil
*400g/14oz can chickpeas, rinsed
and drained*
*200g/7oz can cannellini beans, rinsed
and drained*
*150ml/¹/4 pint/²/3 cup passata (bottled
strained tomatoes)*
120ml/4fl oz/¹/2 cup water
*1.5 litres/2¹/2 pints/6¹/4 cups vegetable or
chicken stock*
1 fresh or dried rosemary sprig
200g/7oz/scant 2 cups dried conchiglie
salt and ground black pepper
fresh rosemary leaves, to garnish
15ml/1 tbsp grated fresh Parmesan cheese

SERVES 6

1 Chop the onion, carrots and celery
sticks finely, either in a food processor or
by hand.

2 Heat the olive oil in a large pan, add
the chopped vegetables and cook over
a low heat, stirring frequently, for
5–7 minutes.

3 Add the chickpeas and cannellini
beans, stir well to mix, then cook for
5 minutes. Stir in the passata and water.
Cook, stirring, for 2–3 minutes.

4 Add 475ml/16fl oz/2 cups of the stock,
the rosemary sprig and salt and pepper to
taste. Bring to the boil, cover, then
simmer gently, stirring occasionally, for
1 hour.

NUTRITIONAL NOTES

Per portion:

Energy	201Kcals/849kJ
Total fat	4.5g
Saturated fat	0.9g
Cholesterol	1.84mg
Fibre	3.4g

5 Pour in the remaining stock, add the
pasta and bring to the boil, stirring.
Reduce the heat and simmer, stirring
frequently for 7–8 minutes, or according
to the packet instructions, until the
pasta is tender or al dente. Adjust the
seasoning. Remove and discard the
rosemary sprig and serve the hot soup in
soup bowls, topped with a few rosemary
leaves and a little grated Parmesan.

LENTIL AND PASTA SOUP

This rustic Italian vegetarian soup makes a warming winter meal. It goes well with granary or crusty Italian bread to create a healthy, low-fat supper dish.

INGREDIENTS
175g/6oz/³⁄4 cup brown lentils
3 garlic cloves
1 litre/1³⁄4 pints/4 cups water
15ml/1 tbsp olive oil
1 onion, finely chopped
2 celery sticks, finely chopped
30ml/2 tbsp sun-dried tomato purée (paste)
1.75 litres/3 pints/7¹⁄2 cups vegetable stock
a few fresh marjoram leaves
a few fresh basil leaves
leaves from 1 fresh thyme sprig
*50g/2oz/¹⁄2 cup dried small pasta shapes,
   such as tubetti*
salt and ground black pepper
tiny fresh herb leaves, to garnish

SERVES 6

1 Put the lentils in a large pan. Smash 1 garlic clove (there's no need to peel it first) and add it to the lentils. Pour in the water and bring to the boil. Reduce the heat to a gentle simmer and cook, stirring occasionally, for about 20 minutes or until the lentils are just tender. Tip the lentils into a sieve (strainer), remove the garlic and set it aside. Rinse the lentils under the cold tap, then leave them to drain.

2 Heat the oil in a large pan. Add the onion and celery and cook over a low heat, stirring frequently, for 5–7 minutes until softened.

3 Crush the remaining garlic, then peel and mash the reserved garlic. Add to the vegetables with the tomato purée and the lentils. Stir, then add the stock, the fresh herbs and salt and pepper to taste. Bring to the boil, then simmer for 30 minutes, stirring occasionally.

4 Add the pasta and bring back to the boil, stirring. Simmer, stirring frequently for 7–8 minutes, or according to the packet instructions, until the pasta is tender or al dente. Adjust the seasoning. Serve hot, sprinkled with the herb leaves.

COOK'S TIP
Use green lentils instead of brown if you like, but don't use the orange or red ones as they go mushy.

NUTRITIONAL NOTES
Per portion:

Energy	145Kcals/615kJ
Total fat	3.2g
Saturated fat	0.4g
Cholesterol	0mg
Fibre	3.2g

FRESH TOMATO AND ONION SOUP

—

This delicious wholesome soup is full of flavour and is low in fat too. Serve with slices of
granary bread for a more substantial snack.

INGREDIENTS

10ml/2 tsp sunflower oil
1 large onion, chopped
2 celery sticks, chopped
175g/6oz/3/4 cup split red lentils
*2 large tomatoes, skinned and
roughly chopped*
900ml/1 1/2 pints/3 3/4 cups vegetable stock
*10ml/2 tsp mixed dried Italian herbs, such
as oregano and thyme*
salt and ground black pepper
chopped fresh parsley, to garnish

SERVES 4

1 Heat the oil in a large pan. Add the
chopped onion and celery and cook for
5 minutes, stirring occasionally. Add the
lentils and cook for 1 minute.

2 Stir in the tomatoes, stock, herbs and
seasoning. Cover, bring to the boil and
simmer for about 20 minutes, stirring
occasionally, until the lentils and
vegetables are cooked and tender.
Remove the pan from the heat and set
the soup aside to cool slightly.

3 Purée the soup in a blender or food
processor until smooth. Adjust the
seasoning, return to the rinsed-out pan
and reheat gently until piping hot. Serve
garnished with chopped parsley.

NUTRITIONAL NOTES

Per portion:

Energy	117Kcals/493kJ
Total fat	2.0g
Saturated fat	0.3g
Cholesterol	1mg
Fibre	1.9g

MIXED VEGETABLE SOUP WITH CONCHIGLIETTE

Lean smoked bacon adds delicious flavour to this Italian-style low-fat
vegetable and pasta soup.

3 Add the milk and season with salt and pepper. Purée half of the soup in a blender or food processor until smooth, then return to the pan with the pasta shells. Bring to the boil and simmer for 10 minutes, stirring occasionally.

4 Meanwhile, fry the bacon rashers quickly in a non-stick frying pan for 2–3 minutes until the meat is cooked, stirring frequently. Stir into the soup and ladle into soup bowls to serve. Serve with breadsticks, if you like.

INGREDIENTS

1 small green (bell) pepper
450g/1lb potatoes, peeled and diced
350g/12oz/2 cups canned or frozen corn
1 onion, chopped
1 celery stick, chopped
1 bouquet garni (bay leaf, parsley stalks and thyme)
600ml/1 pint/2½ cups chicken stock
300ml/½ pint/1¼ cups skimmed milk
50g/2oz small dried pasta shells (conchigliette)
115g/4oz lean smoked back bacon rashers (strips), diced
breadsticks, to serve (optional)
salt and ground black pepper

SERVES 6

1 Halve the green pepper and remove and discard the stalk and seeds. Cut the flesh into small dice. Place in a bowl, cover with boiling water and leave to stand for 2 minutes. Rinse and drain.

2 Put the green pepper into a pan with the diced potatoes, corn, onion, celery, bouquet garni and chicken stock. Bring to the boil, cover and simmer for 20 minutes until the vegetables are tender, stirring occasionally.

NUTRITIONAL NOTES

Per portion:

Energy	177Kcals/748kJ
Total fat	3.6g
Saturated fat	1.2g
Cholesterol	10.82mg
Fibre	1.8g

LENTIL SOUP WITH TOMATOES

This classic rustic Italian soup is low in fat and flavoured with rosemary, and is delicious served
with crusty bread or low-fat garlic bread.

INGREDIENTS
225g/8oz/1 cup dried green or
brown lentils
10ml/2 tsp extra virgin olive oil
2 rindless lean back bacon rashers (strips),
cut into small dice
1 onion, finely chopped
2 celery sticks, finely chopped
2 carrots, finely diced
2 fresh rosemary sprigs, finely chopped
2 bay leaves
400g/14oz can chopped plum tomatoes
1.75 litres/3 pints/7½ cups vegetable stock
salt and ground black pepper
fresh bay leaves and rosemary sprigs,
to garnish

SERVES 4

1 Place the lentils in a bowl and cover
with cold water. Leave to soak for 2 hours.
Rinse and drain well.

2 Heat the oil in a large pan. Add the
bacon and cook for about 3 minutes, then
stir in the chopped onion and cook for
5 minutes until softened, stirring
occasionally. Stir in the celery, carrots,
chopped rosemary, bay leaves and lentils.

3 Add the tomatoes and stock and bring
to the boil. Reduce the heat, half cover
the pan, and simmer for about 1 hour, or
until the lentils are perfectly tender,
stirring occasionally.

4 Remove and discard the bay leaves,
add salt and pepper to taste and serve
garnished with bay leaves and rosemary.

NUTRITIONAL NOTES
Per portion:

Energy	235Kcals/995kJ
Total fat	4.9g
Saturated fat	0.9g
Cholesterol	3.48mg
Fibre	6.9g

SPINACH AND RICE SOUP

Use very fresh, young spinach leaves to prepare this light and fresh-tasting low-fat Italian soup.

INGREDIENTS
675g/1½lb fresh spinach, washed
15ml/1 tbsp extra virgin olive oil
1 small onion, finely chopped
2 garlic cloves, finely chopped
1 small fresh red chilli, deseeded and
finely chopped
115g/4oz/generous ½ cup risotto rice
1.2 litres/2 pints/5 cups vegetable stock
salt and ground black pepper
20ml/4 tsp grated fresh Pecorino cheese,
to serve

SERVES 4

1 Place the spinach in a large pan with
just the water clinging to the leaves. Add
a large pinch of salt and heat gently until
wilted. Remove from the heat and drain,
reserving any liquid.

2 Either chop the spinach finely or place
in a food processor and blend to a purée.

3 Heat the oil in a pan and cook the
onion, garlic and chilli for 4–5 minutes,
stirring occasionally. Stir in the rice, then
the stock and spinach liquid. Boil, then
simmer for 10 minutes. Add the spinach
and seasoning and cook for 5–7 minutes.
Serve with the Pecorino cheese.

NUTRITIONAL NOTES
Per portion:

Energy	235Kcals/995kJ
Total fat	4.9g
Saturated fat	0.9g
Cholesterol	3.48mg
Fibre	6.9g

CONSOMMÉ WITH AGNOLOTTI

—

A flavourful Italian pasta soup, ideal for a tasty appetizer or snack.

INGREDIENTS

*75g/3oz cooked, peeled prawns (shrimp),
plus 50g/2oz to garnish
75g/3oz canned crab meat, drained
5ml/1 tsp fresh root ginger, peeled and
finely grated
15ml/1 tbsp fresh white breadcrumbs
5ml/1 tsp light soy sauce
1 spring onion (scallion), finely chopped
1 garlic clove, crushed
1 quantity of basic pasta dough
(see Techniques section)
egg white, beaten
400g/14oz can chicken or fish consommé
30ml/2 tbsp sherry or vermouth
salt and ground black pepper
fresh coriander (cilantro), to garnish*

SERVES 6

1 Put the prawns, crab meat, ginger, breadcrumbs, soy sauce, onion, garlic and seasoning into a blender or food processor and blend until smooth. Set aside.

2 Roll the pasta into thin sheets. Stamp out 32 rounds 5cm/2in in diameter, with a fluted pastry (cookie) cutter.

3 Place a small teaspoon of the puréed filling in the centre of half the pasta rounds. Brush the edges of each round with egg white and sandwich together by placing a second pasta round on top. Pinch the edges together firmly to stop the filling seeping out.

4 Cook the pasta in a large pan of boiling, salted water for 5 minutes (cook in batches to stop them sticking together). Remove from the pan and drop into a bowl of cold water for 5 seconds before removing and placing on a tray.

5 Heat the chicken or fish consommé in a pan with the sherry or vermouth. When piping hot, add the cooked pasta shapes and simmer for 1–2 minutes.

6 Serve the cooked pasta in shallow soup bowls covered with hot consommé. Garnish with prawns and coriander.

NUTRITIONAL NOTES

Per portion:

Energy	177Kcals/747kJ
Total fat	2.7g
Saturated fat	0.7g
Cholesterol	89.66mg
Fibre	1g

COOK'S TIP

You can make these pasta shapes a day in advance. Cover with clear film (plastic wrap) and store in the refrigerator.

APPETIZERS, SALADS AND SNACKS

This APPETIZING *array of low-fat Italian recipes provides tempting dishes to launch a meal,* HEALTHY *and* REFRESHING *salads and tasty low-fat snacks to enjoy at any time of the day. Choose from* ITALIAN *dishes such as Aubergine, Garlic and* PEPPER *Pâté,* ROCKET, *Pear and Parmesan Salad, Tomato Pesto Toasties and* PROSCIUTTO *and Pepper Pizzas.*

AUBERGINE SUNFLOWER PÂTÉ

—

This delicious aubergine pâté, flavoured with sunflower seeds and fresh herbs, makes a tempting low-fat appetizer or snack.

INGREDIENTS

1 large aubergine (eggplant)
1 garlic clove, crushed
15ml/1 tbsp lemon juice
30ml/2 tbsp sunflower seeds
45ml/3 tbsp low-fat natural (plain) yogurt
handful of fresh coriander (cilantro) or
parsley, plus extra to garnish
ground black pepper
vegetable sticks, to serve

SERVES 4

1 Cut the aubergine in half and place, cut side down, on a baking sheet. Place under a hot grill (broiler) for 15–20 minutes, until the skin is blackened and the flesh is soft.

2 Leave for a few minutes to cool slightly, then scoop the flesh into a blender or food processor. Discard the skin. Add the garlic, lemon juice, sunflower seeds and yogurt to the processor. Blend together until smooth.

3 Roughly chop the fresh coriander or parsley and mix into the aubergine mixture. Season with black pepper, then spoon into a serving dish. Garnish with coriander or parsley and serve with vegetable sticks.

NUTRITIONAL NOTES

Per portion:

Energy	59Kcals/245kJ
Total fat	4g
Saturated fat	0.5g
Cholesterol	0.44mg
Fibre	1.5g

PEPPER DIPS WITH CRUDITÉS

—

Make one or both of these colourful Italian vegetable dips – if you have time to make both they look spectacular together and are both low-fat too!

INGREDIENTS

2 red (bell) peppers, halved and deseeded
2 yellow (bell) peppers, halved
and deseeded
2 garlic cloves
30ml/2 tbsp lemon juice
20ml/4 tsp olive oil
50g/2oz/1 cup fresh white breadcrumbs
salt and ground black pepper
prepared fresh vegetables,
for dipping

SERVES 6

1 Place the peppers in two separate pans with a peeled clove of garlic. Add just enough water to cover.

2 Bring to the boil, then cover and simmer for 15 minutes until tender. Drain, cool, then purée the peppers separately in a blender or food processor, adding half the lemon juice and olive oil to each purée.

3 Stir half the breadcrumbs into each purée and season to taste with salt and pepper. Spoon the dips into serving dishes, garnish with a grinding of black pepper and serve with a selection of fresh vegetables for dipping.

NUTRITIONAL NOTES

Per portion:

Energy	60Kcals/253kJ
Total fat	3g
Saturated fat	0.5g
Cholesterol	0mg
Fibre	1.1g

AUBERGINE, GARLIC AND PEPPER PÂTÉ

Serve this Italian-style chunky, garlicky pâté of smoky baked aubergine and red peppers on a
bed of salad, accompanied by crispbreads.

INGREDIENTS

3 aubergines (eggplants)
2 red (bell) peppers
5 garlic cloves
7.5ml/1 1/2 tsp pink peppercorns in brine,
drained and crushed
30ml/2 tbsp chopped fresh coriander
(cilantro)

SERVES 4

NUTRITIONAL NOTES

Per portion:

Energy	15Kcals/64kJ
Total fat	0.4g
Saturated fat	0.1g
Cholesterol	0mg
Fibre	1.8g

1 Preheat the oven to 200°C/400°F/Gas 6.
Arrange the whole aubergines, peppers
and garlic cloves on a baking sheet and
place in the oven. After 10 minutes
remove the garlic cloves. Turn over the
aubergines and peppers and return to
the oven.

2 Carefully peel the garlic cloves and
place them in the bowl of a blender or
food processor.

3 After a further 20 minutes remove the
blistered and charred peppers from the
oven and place in a plastic bag. Leave
to cool.

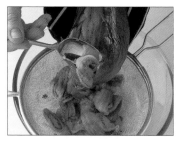

4 After a further 10 minutes remove the
aubergines from the oven. Split in half
and scoop the flesh into a sieve (strainer)
placed over a bowl. Discard the skin.
Press the flesh with a spoon to remove the
bitter juices. Discard the juices.

5 Add the aubergine flesh to the garlic in
the blender or food processor and blend
until smooth. Place in a large bowl.

6 Peel and chop the red peppers and stir
into the aubergine mixture. Mix in the
peppercorns and fresh coriander, spoon
into a serving dish and serve immediately.

CANNELLINI BEAN PURÉE WITH CHICORY

The slightly bitter flavours of the chicory and radicchio make a wonderful marriage with the
creamy bean purée to create this low-fat appetizer or snack.

3 Cut each radicchio head into eight
wedges. Preheat the grill (broiler).

4 Lay out the chicory and radicchio on a
baking sheet and brush lightly with the
walnut oil. Grill (broil) for 2–3 minutes.
Serve with the bean purée and scatter
over the orange shreds to garnish,
if using.

INGREDIENTS

400g/14oz can cannellini beans
45ml/3 tbsp low-fat fromage frais
finely grated rind and juice of
1 large orange
15ml/1 tbsp finely chopped fresh rosemary
4 heads of chicory (Belgian endive)
2 heads of radicchio
10ml/2 tsp walnut oil
longer shreds of orange rind,
to garnish (optional)

SERVES 4

COOK'S TIP
Other suitable beans to use are haricot
(navy), mung or broad (fava) beans.

1 Drain the beans, rinse, and drain them
again. Purée the beans in a blender or
food processor with the fromage frais,
orange rind and juice and rosemary.
Set aside.

2 Cut the heads of chicory in half along
the length.

NUTRITIONAL NOTES
Per portion:

Energy	142Kcals/602kJ
Total fat	3.4g
Saturated fat	0.5g
Cholesterol	0.11mg
Fibre	1.1g

ROASTED PLUM TOMATOES WITH GARLIC

—

A very typical Italian dish, these roast tomatoes flavoured with garlic are so simple to prepare,
yet taste absolutely wonderful. A shallow earthenware dish will allow the tomatoes to char.

INGREDIENTS

8 plum tomatoes
12 garlic cloves
20ml/4 tsp extra virgin olive oil
3 bay leaves
salt and ground black pepper
45ml/3 tbsp fresh oregano leaves,
to garnish

SERVES 4

1 Preheat the oven to 230°C/450°F/Gas 8.
Cut the plum tomatoes in half, leaving a
small part of the green stem intact for the
final decoration.

2 Select an ovenproof dish that will
hold all the tomatoes snugly together in a
single layer. Place them in the dish with
the cut side facing upwards, and push
each of the whole, unpeeled garlic cloves
among them.

3 Lightly brush the tomatoes with the oil,
add the bay leaves and sprinkle black
pepper over the top.

4 Bake in the oven for about 35–45
minutes until the tomatoes have softened
and are sizzling in the dish. They should
be charred around the edges. Season with
salt and a little more black pepper, if
needed. Garnish with the fresh oregano
leaves and serve immediately.

COOK'S TIP

Select ripe, juicy tomatoes without any
blemishes to get the best flavour.

VARIATION

For a sweet alternative, use halved and
seeded red or yellow (bell) peppers
instead of the tomatoes.

NUTRITIONAL NOTES

Per portion:

Energy	57Kcals/238kJ
Total fat	4.0g
Saturated fat	0.6g
Cholesterol	0mg
Fibre	1.1g

ARTICHOKE SALAD WITH SALSA AGRODOLCE
—

Agrodolce is an Italian sweet-and-sour sauce which makes an ideal accompaniment for this
artichoke and bean salad.

INGREDIENTS
6 small globe artichokes
juice of 1 lemon
15ml/1 tbsp olive oil
2 onions, roughly chopped
175g/6oz/1 cup fresh or frozen broad
(fava) beans (shelled weight)
175g/6oz/1 1/2 cups fresh or frozen peas
(shelled weight)
salt and ground black pepper
fresh mint leaves, to garnish

FOR THE SALSA AGRODOLCE
120ml/4fl oz/1/2 cup white wine vinegar
15ml/1 tbsp caster (superfine) sugar
handful of fresh mint leaves, roughly torn

SERVES 4–6

1 Peel and discard the outer leaves from
the artichokes and cut into quarters.
Place the artichokes in a bowl of water
with the lemon juice.

2 Heat the oil in a large pan and add the
onions. Cook until the onions are golden,
stirring occasionally. Add the broad
beans and stir, then drain the artichokes
and add to the pan. Pour in about
300ml/1/2 pint/1 1/4 cups of water, bring
to the boil, then cook, covered, for
10–15 minutes.

3 Add the peas, season with salt and
pepper and cook for a further 5 minutes,
stirring occasionally, until the vegetables
are tender. Strain through a sieve
(strainer), discard the liquid, then
place all the vegetables in a bowl, leave
to cool, cover and chill.

4 To make the salsa agrodolce, mix
all the ingredients in a pan. Heat gently
for 2–3 minutes until the sugar has
dissolved. Simmer for 5 minutes, stirring
occasionally. Remove from the heat and
let cool. To serve, drizzle the salsa over
the vegetables and garnish with mint leaves.

NUTRITIONAL NOTES
Per portion:

Energy	182Kcals/759kJ
Total fat	4g
Saturated fat	0.6g
Cholesterol	0mg
Fibre	5.5g

GARLIC BAKED TOMATOES
—

For the best results, use Italian plum tomatoes, which have a warm, slightly sweet flavour.
Serve this tasty dish with fresh Italian bread or crispbreads.

INGREDIENTS
25g/1oz/2 tbsp unsalted butter
1 large garlic clove, crushed
5ml/1 tsp finely grated orange rind
*4 firm plum tomatoes, or 2 large
beef tomatoes*
salt and ground black pepper
fresh basil leaves, to garnish

SERVES 4

1 Soften the butter in a small bowl and
blend with the crushed garlic, orange rind,
and seasoning. Chill for a few minutes.

2 Preheat the oven to 200°C/400°F/Gas 6.
Halve the tomatoes crossways and trim
the bases so they stand upright.

3 Place the tomatoes in an ovenproof dish
and spread the butter equally over each.

4 Bake the tomatoes in the oven for
15–25 minutes, depending on the size of
the tomato halves, until just tender. Serve
sprinkled with the fresh basil leaves.

NUTRITIONAL NOTES
Per portion:

Energy	49Kcals/204kJ
Total fat	5g
Saturated fat	3.3g
Cholesterol	13.88mg
Fibre	0.3g

LEMON CARROT SALAD
—

This tangy, colourful and refreshing salad creates an ideal low-fat snack or accompaniment.

INGREDIENTS
450g/1lb small, young carrots
finely grated rind and juice of 1/2 lemon
15ml/1 tbsp soft light brown sugar
30ml/2 tbsp sunflower oil
5ml/1 tsp hazelnut or sesame oil
5ml/1 tsp chopped fresh oregano
salt and ground black pepper

SERVES 6

NUTRITIONAL NOTES
Per portion:

Energy	76Kcals/318kJ
Total fat	4.7g
Saturated fat	0.6g
Cholesterol	0mg
Fibre	1.8g

1 Finely grate the carrots and place them
in a large bowl. Stir in the lemon rind and
15–30ml/1–2 tbsp of the lemon juice.

2 Add the sugar, sunflower and hazelnut
or sesame oils, and mix well. Add more
lemon juice and seasoning to taste, then
sprinkle on the oregano and toss lightly
to mix. Leave the salad for 1 hour before
serving, garnished with a sprig of oregano.

VARIATION
Experiment with different herbs.
Tarragon goes well with carrots.

1
w
pa
th
u

THREE-COLOUR SALAD

—

This classic Italian dish, *insalata tricolore*, creates a tasty and colourful appetizer
or snack. Use plum or vine-ripened tomatoes for the best flavour.

INGREDIENTS

1 small red onion,
thinly sliced
6 large full-flavoured tomatoes
50g/2oz/1 small bunch rocket (arugula)
or watercress, roughly chopped
115g/4oz reduced-fat mozzarella cheese,
thinly sliced or grated
20ml/4 tsp extra virgin
olive oil
30ml/2 tbsp pine nuts
(optional)
salt and ground black pepper

SERVES 6

1 Soak the onion slices in a bowl of
cold water for 30 minutes, then drain
and pat dry.

2 Prepare the tomatoes for skinning by
slashing them with a sharp knife and
dipping briefly in boiling water.

3 Peel off the skins and then slice each
tomato using a sharp knife.

4 Arrange half the tomato slices on a
large platter, or divide them among six
small plates if you prefer.

5 Layer with half the chopped rocket
or watercress and half the onion slices,
seasoning well. Add half the cheese,
sprinkling over a little more seasoning
as you go.

6 Repeat with the remaining tomato and
onion slices, salad leaves and cheese.

7 Season well to finish and sprinkle the
oil over the salad. Scatter the pine nuts
over the top, if using. Cover the salad and
chill for at least 2 hours before serving.

NUTRITIONAL NOTES

Per portion:

Energy	75Kcals/314kJ
Total fat	5g
Saturated fat	2g
Cholesterol	7.36mg
Fibre	0.6g

VARIATIONS

Instead of the fresh rocket or
watercress, use chopped fresh basil,
which goes particularly well with the
flavour of ripe tomatoes. To reduce
the fat content even further, omit the
oil and sprinkle the salad with
a fat-free vinaigrette dressing.

ROASTED PEPPER AND TOMATO SALAD

This recipe brings together perfectly the colours, flavours and textures of southern Italian food.
Serve this low-fat dish at room temperature with a green salad.

INGREDIENTS
3 red (bell) peppers
6 large plum tomatoes
2.5ml/¹/₂ tsp dried red chilli flakes
1 red onion, thinly sliced
3 garlic cloves, finely chopped
finely grated rind and juice of 1 lemon
45ml/3 tbsp chopped fresh flat leaf parsley
20ml/4 tsp extra virgin olive oil
salt and ground black pepper
25g/1oz black and green olives and extra
chopped fresh flat leaf parsley, to garnish

SERVES 4

1 Preheat the oven to 220°C/425°F/Gas 7. Place the peppers on a baking sheet and roast in the oven, turning occasionally, for 10 minutes or until the skins are almost blackened. Add the tomatoes to the baking sheet and bake for a further 5 minutes.

2 Place the peppers in a plastic bag, close the top loosely, trapping in the steam, and then set them aside with the tomatoes until they are cool enough to handle.

3 Carefully pull off and discard the skin from the peppers. Remove and discard the seeds, then chop the peppers and tomatoes roughly and place them together in a mixing bowl.

4 Add the chilli flakes, onion, garlic, lemon rind and juice. Sprinkle over the parsley. Mix well, then transfer to a serving dish. Sprinkle with a little salt and pepper, drizzle over the olive oil and scatter the olives and extra parsley over the top to garnish. Serve the salad at room temperature.

NUTRITIONAL NOTES
Per portion:

Energy	78Kcals/323kJ
Total fat	4.9g
Saturated fat	0.8g
Cholesterol	0mg
Fibre	2.1g

MARINATED COURGETTES

This is a simple vegetable dish which is prepared all over Italy using the best of the season's
courgettes. It can be eaten hot or cold and creates a delicious accompaniment to a main course.

INGREDIENTS
4 courgettes (zucchini)
40ml/8 tsp extra virgin olive oil
30ml/2 tbsp chopped fresh mint, plus
whole leaves, to garnish
30ml/2 tbsp white wine vinegar
salt and ground black pepper

SERVES 6

1 Cut the courgettes into thin slices. Heat 20ml/4 tsp of the oil in a wide heavy pan.

2 Fry the courgettes in batches, for 4–6 minutes, until tender and brown around the edges. Transfer the courgettes to a bowl. Season well.

NUTRITIONAL NOTES
Per portion:

Energy	50Kcals/206KJ
Total fat	5.0g
Saturated fat	0.7g
Cholesterol	0mg
Fibre	0.3g

3 Heat the remaining oil, then add the mint and vinegar and let bubble for a few seconds. Stir into the courgettes. Marinate for 1 hour, then serve with mint leaves.

DUCK BREAST SALAD

Succulent duck breasts are grilled, then sliced and tossed together with pasta and fruit in a
delicious virtually fat-free dressing to create this tempting salad.

INGREDIENTS

2 duck breasts, boned
5ml/1 tsp coriander seeds, crushed
350g/12oz dried rigatoni
150ml/¼ pint/⅔ cup fresh orange juice
15ml/1 tbsp lemon juice
10ml/2 tsp clear honey
1 shallot, finely chopped
1 garlic clove, crushed
1 celery stick, chopped
75g/3oz dried cherries
45ml/3 tbsp port or red wine
15ml/1 tbsp chopped fresh mint, plus extra
to garnish
30ml/2 tbsp chopped fresh coriander
(cilantro), plus extra to garnish
1 eating apple, cored and diced
2 oranges, segmented
salt and ground black pepper

SERVES 6

1 Remove and discard the skin and fat
from the duck breasts and season with
salt and pepper. Rub the duck breasts
all over with crushed coriander seeds.
Preheat the grill (broiler), then grill
(broil) the duck for 7–10 minutes
depending on size. Wrap in foil and set
aside for about 20 minutes.

2 Meanwhile, cook the pasta in a large
pan of boiling, salted water until tender or
al dente. Drain thoroughly and rinse
under cold running water, then drain
again. Leave to cool.

3 In the meantime, make the dressing.
Put the orange juice, lemon juice, honey,
shallot, garlic, celery, cherries, port or red
wine, chopped mint and coriander into a
bowl, whisk together then set aside for
20–30 minutes.

NUTRITIONAL NOTES

Per portion:

Energy	298Kcals/1266kJ
Total fat	2.3g
Saturated fat	0.5g
Cholesterol	27.5mg
Fibre	3g

4 Slice the duck very thinly. (It should be
pink in the centre.)

5 Put the pasta into a bowl, add the duck,
dressing, diced apple and segments of
orange. Toss well to mix. Transfer the
salad to a serving plate and garnish with
the extra mint and coriander. Serve.

COOK'S TIP

To skin the duck breasts, slide your
fingers between the skin and breast
and gently pull to separate. Use a sharp
knife to loosen any stubborn parts.

VARIATION

Other shapes of pasta may be
substituted for the rigatoni. Penne work
well, although long varieties, such as
tagliatelle, are also good.

SPICY CHICKEN SALAD

—

This tasty Italian-style low-fat chicken and pasta salad creates an ideal lunch or
supper dish for family or friends.

INGREDIENTS

5ml/1 tsp ground cumin seeds
5ml/1 tsp ground paprika
5ml/1 tsp ground turmeric
1–2 garlic cloves, crushed
45–60ml/3–4 tbsp fresh lime juice
*4 small chicken breasts, boned
and skinned*
225g/8oz dried rigatoni
1 red (bell) pepper, deseeded and chopped
2 celery sticks, thinly sliced
1 shallot or small onion, finely chopped
15g/¹/₂oz stuffed green olives, halved
30ml/2 tbsp clear honey
10ml/2 tsp wholegrain mustard
salt and ground black pepper
mixed salad leaves, to serve

SERVES 6

1 Mix the cumin, paprika, turmeric,
garlic, seasoning and 30ml/2 tbsp lime
juice in a bowl. Lay the chicken in a
shallow non-metallic dish and rub the
mixture over the chicken breasts. Cover
with clear film (plastic wrap) and leave in
a cool place for about 3 hours or overnight.

2 Preheat the oven to 200°C/400°F/Gas 6.
Put the chicken on a grill (broiling) rack in
a single layer and bake in the oven for
20 minutes until cooked. (Alternatively,
grill (broil) for 8–10 minutes on each side.)

3 Meanwhile, cook the rigatoni in a large
pan of boiling, salted water until tender or
al dente. Drain and rinse under cold
water. Leave to drain thoroughly.

4 Put the red pepper, celery, shallot or
onion and olives into a large bowl with
the pasta and toss to mix.

5 Mix the honey, mustard and remaining
lime juice together in a bowl and pour
over the pasta. Toss to mix well.

6 Cut the chicken into bite-size pieces.
Arrange the mixed salad leaves on a
serving dish, spoon the pasta mixture in
the centre of the leaves and top with the
spicy chicken pieces.

NUTRITIONAL NOTES
Per portion:

Energy	234Kcals/993kJ
Total fat	4g
Saturated fat	1.1g
Cholesterol	37.88mg
Fibre	1.6g

TOMATO PESTO TOASTIES

Ready-made pesto is high in fat but, as its flavour is so powerful, it can be used in very small
amounts with good effect, as in these tasty low-fat toasties.

3 Cut the tomato and onion, crossways,
into thin slices using a large sharp knife.

4 Arrange the tomato and onion slices,
overlapping, on top of the toast and
season. Cook under a hot grill until
heated through, then serve, garnished
with a sprig of thyme.

INGREDIENTS
2 thick slices of crusty bread
45ml/3 tbsp skimmed milk soft cheese or
low-fat fromage frais
10ml/2 tsp red or green pesto
1 beef tomato
1 red onion
salt and ground black pepper

SERVES 2

1 Toast the bread slices under a hot grill
(broiler) until golden brown on both sides,
turning once. Leave to cool.

2 Mix together the soft cheese or fromage
frais and pesto in a small bowl until well
blended, then spread thickly on to the
toasted bread.

COOK'S TIP
Almost any type of crusty bread can be
used, but Italian ciabatta and French
bread give the best flavour.

NUTRITIONAL NOTES
Per portion:

Energy	149Kcals/629kJ
Total fat	4g
Saturated fat	1g
Cholesterol	2.57mg
Fibre	1.2g

PROSCIUTTO AND PEPPER PIZZAS

—

The delicious flavours of these quick and easy Italian pizza snacks are hard to beat.
Serve with mixed salad leaves and sliced plum tomatoes.

INGREDIENTS

1/2 loaf of ciabatta bread
1 red (bell) pepper, roasted, peeled
and deseeded
1 yellow (bell) pepper, roasted, peeled
and deseeded
4 thin slices prosciutto, cut into thick strips
50g/2oz reduced-fat mozzarella cheese
ground black pepper
tiny fresh basil leaves,
to garnish

MAKES 4

3 Thinly slice the mozzarella and arrange
on top, then grind over plenty of black
pepper. Grill (broil) for 2–3 minutes until
the cheese is bubbling.

NUTRITIONAL NOTES
Per portion:

Energy	213Kcals/903kJ
Total fat	3.9g
Saturated fat	1.67g
Cholesterol	8.76mg
Fibre	1.5

4 Scatter the basil leaves on top to
garnish and serve immediately.

1 Cut the bread into four thick slices and
toast until golden.

2 Cut the roasted peppers into thick
strips and arrange on the toasted bread
with the strips of prosciutto. Preheat
the grill (broiler).

MEAT, POULTRY
AND
FISH DISHES

WHITE FISH *is naturally low in fat*
and by choosing LEAN CUTS *of meat*
and poultry these foods can be ENJOYED
as part of a HEALTHY *low-fat diet.*
Choose from this nourishing collection of
low-fat Italian MAIN COURSE *meat,*
poultry and fish dishes including
PANCETTA *and Bean* RISOTTO,
Tuscan Chicken and Roast Monkfish with
GARLIC *and Fennel.*

FILLET OF BEEF WITH HERBY TAGLIATELLE

This Italian-style fillet of beef served with herby pasta creates a delicious
low-fat main course or supper dish.

INGREDIENTS
450g/1lb lean beef fillet
*450g/1lb fresh tagliatelle made with
sun-dried tomatoes and herbs*
115g/4oz cherry tomatoes
1/2 cucumber

FOR THE MARINADE
15ml/1 tbsp soy sauce
15ml/1 tbsp sherry
*5ml/1 tsp fresh root ginger, peeled
and grated*
1 garlic clove, crushed

FOR THE HERB DRESSING
*150ml/1/4 pint/2/3 cup low-fat natural
(plain) yogurt*
1 garlic clove, crushed
*30–45ml/2–3 tbsp chopped fresh herbs
(chives, parsley, thyme)*
salt and ground black pepper

SERVES 6

1 Mix all the marinade ingredients
together in a shallow non-metallic dish,
put the beef in and turn it over to coat it.
Cover with clear film (plastic wrap) and
leave for 30 minutes to allow the flavours
to penetrate the meat. Preheat the
grill (broiler).

2 Lift the fillet out of the marinade and
pat it dry with kitchen paper. Grill (broil)
on a grill (broiling) rack for 8 minutes on
each side, basting with the marinade.

3 Transfer to a plate, cover with foil and
leave to stand for 20 minutes.

4 Mix the dressing ingredients thoroughly.
Cook the pasta in a large pan of lightly
salted boiling water, according to the
packet instructions, until tender or
al dente. Drain thoroughly, rinse under
cold water and drain again.

5 Cut the cherry tomatoes in half. Cut the
cucumber in half lengthways, scoop out
and discard the seeds with a teaspoon
and slice the flesh thinly into crescents.

6 Put the pasta, cherry tomatoes,
cucumber and dressing into a bowl and
toss to mix well. Slice the beef thinly and
arrange on serving plates with the pasta
salad served alongside.

NUTRITIONAL NOTES
Per portion:

Energy	201Kcals/848kJ
Total fat	4.3g
Saturated fat	1.7g
Cholesterol	45.25mg
Fibre	1.2g

VEAL WITH TOMATOES AND WHITE WINE
—

This famous Milanese dish is delicious and hearty and creates an ideal main course
meal for special occasions. It goes very well with a green salad.

INGREDIENTS
30ml/2 tbsp plain (all-purpose) flour
4 pieces of lean veal shank
2 small onions
10ml/2 tsp olive oil
1 large celery stick,
finely chopped
1 carrot, finely chopped
2 garlic cloves, finely chopped
400g/14oz can chopped tomatoes
300ml/¹/2 pint/1¹/4 cups dry
white wine
300ml/¹/2 pint/1¹/4 cups chicken or
veal stock
1 strip of thinly pared lemon rind
2 bay leaves, plus extra for garnishing
salt and ground black pepper

FOR THE GREMOLATA
30ml/2 tbsp finely chopped fresh flat
leaf parsley
finely grated rind of 1 lemon
1 garlic clove, finely chopped

SERVES 4

1 Preheat the oven to 160°C/325°F/Gas 3.
Season the flour with salt and pepper and
spread it out in a shallow bowl. Add the
pieces of veal and turn them in the flour
until they are evenly coated. Shake off
any excess flour.

2 Slice one of the onions into rings. Heat
the olive oil in a large flameproof
casserole, then add the veal pieces, with
the onion rings, and brown the veal on
both sides over a medium heat. Remove
the veal with tongs, place on a plate and
set aside to drain.

3 Chop the remaining onion and add to
the pan with the celery, carrot and garlic.
Stir the bottom of the pan to mix in the
juices and sediment. Cook gently, stirring
frequently, for about 5 minutes until the
vegetables soften slightly.

4 Add the tomatoes, wine, stock, lemon
rind and bay leaves, then season to taste
with salt and pepper. Bring the mixture to
the boil, stirring.

5 Return the veal pieces to the pan and
stir to coat thoroughly with the sauce.
Cover and cook in the oven for 2 hours or
until the veal feels tender when pierced
with a fork.

6 Meanwhile, make the gremolata. Mix
together the parsley, lemon rind and
garlic in a small bowl. Remove the
casserole from the oven and discard the
lemon rind and bay leaves. Adjust the
seasoning. Serve hot, sprinkled with the
gremolata and garnished with bay leaves.

NUTRITIONAL NOTES
Per portion:

Energy	219Kcals/919kJ
Total fat	4.8g
Saturated fat	1.2g
Cholesterol	84.8mg
Fibre	1.3g

PANCETTA AND BEAN RISOTTO

This delicious Italian risotto makes a healthy and filling low-fat meal, served with cooked fresh
seasonal vegetables or a mixed green salad.

INGREDIENTS
10ml/2 tsp olive oil
1 onion, chopped
2 garlic cloves, finely chopped
*115g/4oz smoked pancetta or smoked lean
back bacon, diced*
350g/12oz/1¾ cups risotto rice
*1.5 litres/2½ pints/6¼ cups simmering
chicken stock*
*225g/8oz/1⅓ cups frozen baby broad
(fava) beans*
*30ml/2 tbsp chopped fresh mixed herbs,
such as parsley, thyme and oregano*
salt and ground black pepper
shaved fresh Parmesan cheese, to serve

SERVES 6

1 Heat the oil in a large pan. Add the
onion, garlic and pancetta or bacon and
cook gently for about 5 minutes, stirring
occasionally. Do not allow the onion and
garlic to brown.

2 Add the rice and cook for 1 minute,
stirring. Add a ladleful of stock and
cook, stirring, until absorbed.

3 Add more ladlefuls of stock until the
rice is tender and almost all the liquid
absorbed. This will take 30–35 minutes.
Meanwhile, cook the broad beans in
salted, boiling water for about 3 minutes.
Drain and stir into the risotto, with the
herbs. Season to taste. Sprinkle with
shavings of Parmesan cheese.

NUTRITIONAL NOTES
Per portion:

Energy	294Kcals/1250kJ
Total fat	5g
Saturated fat	1.6g
Cholesterol	8.5mg
Fibre	2.7g

HUNTER'S CHICKEN
—

This traditional Italian dish combines chicken in a flavourful tomato, mushroom and herb sauce
to create a tempting main course, ideal served with mashed potatoes or cooked polenta.

3 Add the onion and chopped porcini
mushrooms to the pan. Cook gently,
stirring frequently, for about 3 minutes
until the onion has softened but not
browned. Stir in the chopped tomatoes,
wine and reserved mushroom soaking
liquid, then add the crushed garlic and
chopped rosemary, with salt and pepper
to taste. Bring to the boil, stirring all
the time.

INGREDIENTS

15g/¹/₂oz/¹/₄ cup dried porcini mushrooms
10ml/2 tsp olive oil
*4 small chicken portions, on the
bone, skinned*
1 large onion, thinly sliced
400g/14oz can chopped tomatoes
150ml/¹/₄ pint/²/₃ cup red wine
1 garlic clove, crushed
*leaves of 1 sprig of fresh rosemary,
finely chopped*
*115g/4oz/1³/₄ cups fresh field (portobello)
mushrooms, thinly sliced*
salt and ground black pepper
fresh rosemary sprigs, to garnish

SERVES 4

1 Put the porcini in a bowl, add 250ml/
8fl oz/1 cup warm water and leave to
soak for 20–30 minutes. Remove from
the liquid and squeeze over the bowl.
Strain the liquid and reserve. Finely chop
the porcini.

2 Heat the oil in a large flameproof
casserole. Add the chicken. Sauté over a
medium heat for 5 minutes, or until
golden. Remove and drain on absorbent
kitchen paper.

4 Return the chicken to the pan and turn
to coat it with the sauce. Cover and
simmer gently for 30 minutes.

5 Add the fresh mushrooms and stir
well to mix into the sauce. Continue
simmering gently for 10 minutes or
until the chicken is tender. Adjust the
seasoning to taste. Serve hot, garnished
with fresh rosemary sprigs.

NUTRITIONAL NOTES
Per portion:

Energy	190Kcals/801kJ
Total fat	5g
Saturated fat	1.3g
Cholesterol	44.12mg
Fibre	1.2g

TUSCAN CHICKEN

This simple Italian peasant casserole has all the flavours of traditional Tuscan ingredients and creates a delicious, low-fat supper dish.

3 Lower the heat and simmer gently, stirring occasionally, for 30–35 minutes or until the chicken is tender and the juices run clear, not pink, when pierced with the point of a knife.

4 Stir in the cannellini beans and simmer for a further 5 minutes until heated through. Sprinkle with the breadcrumbs and cook under a hot grill (broiler) until golden brown. Serve immediately, garnished with fresh oregano sprigs.

INGREDIENTS
8 chicken thighs, skinned
5ml/1 tsp olive oil
1 onion, thinly sliced
2 red (bell) peppers, deseeded and sliced
1 garlic clove, crushed
300ml/¹/2 pint/1¹/4 cups passata (bottled strained tomatoes)
150ml/¹/4 pint/²/3 cup dry white wine
a large sprig of fresh oregano, chopped, or 5ml/1 tsp dried oregano
400g/14oz can cannellini beans, drained
45ml/3 tbsp fresh breadcrumbs
salt and ground black pepper
fresh oregano sprigs, to garnish

SERVES 6

1 Fry the chicken in the oil in a non-stick or heavy pan until golden brown all over. Remove from the pan, place on a plate and keep hot. Add the onion and peppers to the pan and gently sauté until softened, but not brown. Add the garlic.

2 Add the chicken, passata, wine and oregano and stir. Season well and bring to the boil, stirring, then cover the pan tightly.

NUTRITIONAL NOTES
Per portion:

Energy	256Kcals/1083kJ
Total fat	4.8g
Saturated fat	1.3g
Cholesterol	49.3mg
Fibre	1.1g

CHICKEN IN A SALT CRUST

Cooking food in a casing of salt gives a deliciously moist, tender flavour that, surprisingly, is not too salty. Serve with a selection of cooked fresh seasonal vegetables.

INGREDIENTS
1.75kg/4–4¹/₂lb chicken
about 2.25kg/5¹/₄lb coarse sea salt

SERVES 6

1 Preheat the oven to 220°C/425°F/Gas 7. Choose a deep ovenproof dish into which the whole chicken will fit snugly. Line the dish with a double thickness of heavy foil, allowing plenty of foil to overhang it.

2 Truss the chicken tightly so that the salt cannot fall into the cavity. Place the chicken on a thin layer of salt in the dish.

COOK'S TIP
This recipe makes a stunning and unusual main course. Garnish the salt-encrusted chicken with fresh mixed herbs and take to the table. Scrape away the salt and transfer to a clean plate to carve.

3 Pour the remaining salt all around and over the top of the chicken until it is completely encased. Sprinkle the top with a little water.

4 Cover tightly with the foil and bake the chicken on the lower shelf in the oven for 1³/4 hours until the chicken is cooked and tender.

5 To serve the chicken, open out the foil and ease it out of the dish. Place on a large serving platter. Crack open the salt crust on the chicken and brush away the salt. Remove and discard the skin from the chicken and carve the meat into slices. Serve.

NUTRITIONAL NOTES
Per portion:

Energy	156Kcals/659kJ
Total fat	4.4g
Saturated fat	1.3g
Cholesterol	61.6mg
Fibre	0g

PRAWNS IN FRESH TOMATO SAUCE

Fresh prawns are cooked and served in a fresh tomato sauce to create this appetizing
Italian-style low-fat dish.

INGREDIENTS
20ml/4 tsp olive oil
1 onion, finely chopped
1 celery stick, finely chopped
*1 small red (bell) pepper, deseeded
and chopped*
120ml/4fl oz/¹/₂ cup red wine
15ml/1 tbsp wine vinegar
*400g/14oz can plum tomatoes, chopped,
with their juice*
*1kg/2¹/₄lb uncooked prawns (shrimp),
in their shells*
2–3 garlic cloves, finely chopped
*45ml/3 tbsp finely chopped
fresh parsley*
*1 dried chilli, crumbled or
chopped (optional)*
salt and ground black pepper

SERVES 6

1 Heat half the oil in a heavy pan. Add
the onion and cook over a low heat until
soft, stirring occasionally. Stir in the
chopped celery and pepper and cook for
5 minutes. Increase the heat and add the
wine, vinegar and tomatoes. Bring
the mixture to the boil and cook for
5 minutes, stirring occasionally. Reduce
the heat, cover the pan and simmer for
about 30 minutes, until the vegetables
are soft, stirring occasionally.

NUTRITIONAL NOTES
Per portion:

Energy	114Kcals/476kJ
Total fat	3.2g
Saturated fat	0.6g
Cholesterol	49.2mg
Fibre	0.8g

2 Remove the pan from the heat and
allow the vegetable mixture to cool a
little, then purée through a food mill to
make a tomato sauce. Set aside.

3 Shell the prawns. Make a shallow
incision with a small, sharp knife along
the back of each prawn and remove the
long, black vein. Set the prawns aside.

4 Heat the remaining oil in a clean,
heavy pan. Stir in the garlic and parsley,
plus the chilli, if using. Cook over a
medium heat, stirring, until the garlic is
golden. Stir in the prepared tomato sauce
and bring to the boil.

5 Stir in the prepared prawns. Bring the
sauce back to the boil. Reduce the heat
slightly and simmer, stirring occasionally,
until the prawns are pink and stiff: this
will take about 6–8 minutes, depending
on their size. Season to taste and serve.

MEDITERRANEAN FISH CUTLETS

—

These low-fat fish cutlets are ideal served with boiled potatoes, broccoli and carrots for a delicious Italian supper.

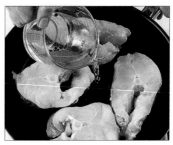

2 Meanwhile, place the fish in a frying pan, pour over the stock and/or wine and add the bay leaf, peppercorns and lemon rind. Cover and simmer for 10 minutes or until the fish is cooked and the flesh flakes easily.

3 Using a slotted spoon, transfer the fish to a heated serving dish. Strain the fish stock into the tomato sauce and boil to reduce slightly. Season the sauce, pour it over the fish and serve immediately, sprinkled with the chopped fresh parsley to garnish.

INGREDIENTS

4 white fish cutlets, about 150g/5oz each
about 150ml/¹/4 pint/²/3 cup fish stock or
dry white wine (or a mixture of the two),
for poaching
1 bay leaf, a few black peppercorns and a
strip of pared lemon rind, for flavouring
chopped fresh parsley, to garnish

FOR THE TOMATO SAUCE
400g/14oz can chopped tomatoes
1 garlic clove, crushed
15ml/1 tbsp pastis or other aniseed-
flavoured liqueur
15ml/1 tbsp drained capers
12–16 pitted black olives
salt and ground black pepper

SERVES 4

1 To make the tomato sauce, place the chopped tomatoes, garlic, pastis or other liqueur, capers and olives in a pan. Season to taste with salt and pepper and cook over a low heat for about 15 minutes, stirring occasionally.

COOK'S TIP

Remove the skin from the fish cutlets and use fewer olives to reduce calories and fat even further. Use 450g/1lb fresh tomatoes, skinned and chopped, in place of canned.

NUTRITIONAL NOTES
Per portion:

Energy	165Kcals/685kJ
Total fat	3.55g
Saturated fat	0.5g
Cholesterol	69mg
Fibre	0.8g

ITALIAN FISH PARCELS

—

Fresh sea bass fillets are topped with mixed Italian vegetables, then barbecued or oven-baked to create this tasty dish, ideal for eating alfresco.

INGREDIENTS

*4 pieces skinless sea bass fillet or 4 whole
small sea bass
10ml/2 tsp olive oil for brushing
2 shallots, thinly sliced
1 garlic clove, chopped
15ml/1 tbsp capers
6 sun-dried tomatoes, finely chopped
4 black olives, pitted and thinly sliced
finely grated rind and juice of 1 lemon
5ml/1 tsp paprika
salt and ground black pepper*

SERVES 4

1 If you are using whole fish, gut them, taking care not to insert the knife too far. Use a teaspoon or your fingers to scrape out the contents. Leave the scales on as they will hold the fragile fish together during cooking.

2 Wash the cavity and the outside of the fish thoroughly with cold water.

3 Cut four large squares of double-thickness foil, large enough to enclose the fish. Brush each square with a little olive oil.

4 Place a piece of fish in the centre of each piece of foil and season well with salt and pepper.

5 Scatter over the shallots, garlic, capers, sun-dried tomatoes, olives and grated lemon rind. Sprinkle with the lemon juice and paprika.

6 Fold the foil over to enclose the fish loosely, sealing the edges firmly so none of the juices can escape.

7 Place on a moderately hot barbecue and cook for 8–10 minutes. Then open up the tops of the parcels and serve.

COOK'S TIPS

• When choosing fish, look for bright, slightly bulging eyes and shiny, faintly slimy skin. Open up the gills to check that they are clear red or dark pink and prod the fish lightly to check that the flesh is springy. All fish should have only a faint, pleasant smell; you can tell a stale fish a mile off by its disagreeable odour.

• Sea bass are prized for their delicate white flesh, and these slim, elegant fish are almost always sold whole. They don't have any irritating small bones, and as a result are never cheap.

NUTRITIONAL NOTES

Per portion:

Energy	117Kcals/492kJ
Total fat	4.5g
Saturated fat	0.6g
Cholesterol	50.2mg
Fibre	0.1g

VARIATIONS

• These parcels can also be baked in the oven: place them on a baking sheet and cook at 200°C/400°F/Gas 6 for 15–20 minutes.

• Sea bass is good for this recipe, but you could also use small whole trout, or white fish fillet such as cod or haddock.

ROAST MONKFISH WITH GARLIC AND FENNEL

Fresh monkfish quickly roasted with garlic and fennel is delicious served with boiled new
potatoes for a summertime Italian meal.

INGREDIENTS

1.2kg/2½lb monkfish tail
8 garlic cloves
15ml/1 tbsp olive oil
2 fennel bulbs, sliced
juice and zest of 1 lemon
1 bay leaf, plus extra
to garnish
salt and ground black pepper

SERVES 6

3 Tie the separated fillets together with
string to reshape as a tailpiece.

6 Place the fish in a roasting dish
together with the fennel slices, lemon
juice, bay leaf and seasoning.

7 Roast in the oven for about 20 minutes,
until tender and cooked through. Serve
immediately, garnished with bay leaves
and lemon zest.

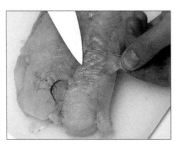

1 Preheat the oven to 220°C/425°F/Gas 7.
With a sharp filleting knife, carefully cut
away the thin membrane covering the
outside of the monkfish; keep the knife
flat against the fish to avoid cutting too
much of the flesh away. When finished,
discard the membrane.

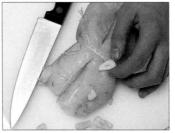

4 Peel and slice the garlic cloves and cut
incisions into the fish flesh. Place the
garlic slices in the incisions.

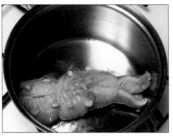

5 Heat the oil in a large, heavy pan and
cook the fish until sealed on all sides.

2 Cut along one side of the central bone
to remove the fillet. Repeat on the other
side. Discard the bone.

COOK'S TIPS

• Monkfish is usually available
all the year round, but if it is not
available then you could substitute
another firm white fish, such as huss.
• The aniseed-like flavour of fennel
goes particularly well with fish.
The leaves can be used as a garnish
if you like.

NUTRITIONAL NOTES

Per portion:

Energy	234Kcals/988kJ
Total fat	4.7g
Saturated fat	0.6g
Cholesterol	123.5mg
Fibre	1.2g

MONKFISH WITH PEPPERED CITRUS MARINADE
—

A fresh citrus fruit marinade adds delicious flavour to monkfish fillets and creates a low-fat,
appetizing dish ideal for cooking and eating alfresco.

INGREDIENTS

2 monkfish tails, about 350g/12oz each
1 lime
1 lemon
2 oranges
a handful of fresh thyme sprigs
20ml/4 tsp olive oil
15ml/1 tbsp mixed peppercorns,
roughly crushed
salt and ground black pepper

SERVES 4

1 Remove and discard any skin from the
monkfish tails.

2 Cut carefully down one side of the
backbone, sliding the knife between the
bone and flesh, to remove the fillet on one
side. (You can ask your fishmonger to do
this for you.)

NUTRITIONAL NOTES
Per portion:

Energy	176Kcals/741kJ
Total fat	5g
Saturated fat	0.7g
Cholesterol	80.6mg
Fibre	0g

3 Turn the fish and repeat on the other
side. Repeat on the second tail. Discard
the bones. Lay the fillets out flat.

4 Cut two slices from each of the citrus
fruits and arrange over two fillets. Add a
few sprigs of thyme and season. Finely
grate the rind from the remaining fruit
and sprinkle over the fish.

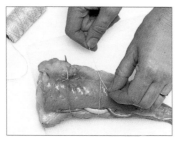

5 Lay the other two fillets on top and tie
them firmly at intervals, with fine cotton
string, to hold them in shape. Place in a
wide, shallow, non-metallic dish.

6 Squeeze the juice from the citrus fruits
and mix it with the oil and more salt and
black pepper.

7 Spoon the juice mixture over the fish.
Cover and leave to marinate for about an
hour, turning occasionally and spooning
the marinade over it.

8 Drain the monkfish, reserving the
marinade, and sprinkle with the crushed
peppercorns. Cook on a medium hot
barbecue for 15–20 minutes, basting the
fish with the marinade and turning it
occasionally, until it is evenly cooked.
Serve immediately.

VARIATION
You can also use this marinade for
monkfish kebabs.

TROUT AND PROSCIUTTO RISOTTO ROLLS

—

This makes a delicious and elegant low-fat meal. The risotto – made with porcini or chanterelle mushrooms and prawns – is an ideal accompaniment for the flavourful trout rolls.

INGREDIENTS
4 trout fillets, skinned
4 thin slices of prosciutto
capers, to garnish

FOR THE RISOTTO
10ml/2 tsp olive oil
8 raw prawns (shrimp), peeled and deveined
1 onion, chopped
225g/8oz/generous 1 cup risotto rice
about 105ml/7 tbsp white wine
about 750ml/1¼ pints/3 cups simmering fish or chicken stock
15g/½oz/2 tbsp dried porcini or chanterelle mushrooms, soaked for 10 minutes in warm water to cover
salt and ground black pepper

SERVES 4

2 Add the onion to the oil in the pan. Fry over a low heat for 3–4 minutes until soft, stirring occasionally. Add the rice and stir for 3–4 minutes until the grains are evenly coated in oil. Add 75ml/5 tbsp of the wine and then the stock, a little at a time, stirring over a gentle heat and allowing the rice to absorb the liquid before adding more.

5 Take a trout fillet, place a spoonful of risotto at one end and roll up. Wrap each fillet in a slice of prosciutto and place in a lightly greased ovenproof dish.

1 First make the risotto. Heat the oil in a heavy pan or deep frying pan and fry the prawns very briefly until flecked with pink, stirring. Lift out using a slotted spoon and transfer to a plate. Set aside.

3 Drain the mushrooms, reserving the liquid, and cut the larger ones in half. Towards the end of cooking, stir the mushrooms into the risotto with 15ml/1 tbsp of the reserved mushroom liquid. If the rice is not yet al dente, add a little more stock or mushroom liquid and cook for 2–3 minutes more. Season to taste with salt and pepper.

4 Remove the pan from the heat and stir in the prawns. Preheat the oven to 190°C/375°F/Gas 5.

6 Spoon any remaining risotto around the fish fillets and sprinkle over the rest of the wine. Bake the rolls in the oven for 15–20 minutes until the fish is cooked and tender. Spoon the risotto on to a platter, top with the trout rolls and garnish with some fat capers. Serve immediately.

COOK'S TIP
Make sure you use proper risotto rice, such as arborio or carnaroli, for this recipe. Short grain rice will not give the right consistency.

NUTRITIONAL NOTES
Per portion:

Energy	245Kcals/1035kJ
Total fat	5g
Saturated fat	1.1g
Cholesterol	63.8mg
Fibre	0.3g

VEGETARIAN
DISHES
AND
VEGETABLES

VEGETARIAN *dishes and vegetables*
play an important part in a LOW-FAT
diet, providing nutritious and filling dishes
made from FRESH INGREDIENTS
that all the family will enjoy. Many of the
dishes are SIMPLE *but substantial and*
provide an enticing menu, including
HERB POLENTA *with Tomatoes,*
Red Pepper Risotto, Stuffed Aubergines
and CAPONATA.

HERB POLENTA WITH TOMATOES

Golden polenta flavoured with fresh summer herbs and served with sweet tomatoes creates this
tasty Italian dish, ideal for lunch or supper.

INGREDIENTS
175g/6oz/1¹/2 cups polenta
750ml/1¹/4 pints/3 cups stock or water
5ml/1 tsp salt
15g/¹/2oz/1 tbsp butter
75ml/5 tbsp mixed chopped
fresh parsley, chives and basil,
plus extra to garnish
10ml/2 tsp olive oil
4 large plum or beef tomatoes, halved
salt and ground black pepper

SERVES 6

1 Prepare the polenta in advance: place
the stock or water in a pan with the salt,
and bring to the boil.

2 Reduce the heat and gradually add the
polenta, stirring all the time to ensure
that it doesn't form any lumps.

NUTRITIONAL NOTES
Per portion:

Energy	185Kcals/773kJ
Total fat	4.7g
Saturated fat	2g
Cholesterol	7mg
Fibre	0.4g

3 Stir constantly over a moderate heat for
5 minutes, until the polenta begins to
thicken and comes away from the sides of
the pan.

4 Remove the pan from the heat and stir
in the butter, herbs and black pepper.

5 Tip the polenta mixture into a wide,
lightly greased dish or tin (pan) and
spread it out evenly. Leave until it is
completely cool and has set.

6 Turn the polenta out on to a board and
cut it into squares or stamp out rounds
with a large biscuit (cookie) cutter. Lightly
brush the squares or rounds with oil.

7 Lightly brush the tomatoes with oil and
sprinkle with salt and pepper.

8 Cook the tomatoes and polenta on a
medium hot barbecue for 5 minutes,
turning once. Serve hot, garnished with
fresh herbs.

VARIATION
Any mixture of fresh herbs can be
used, or try using just basil or chives
alone, for a really distinctive flavour.

POLENTA WITH MUSHROOMS

This low-fat Italian dish is delicious made with a mixture of fresh wild and cultivated mushrooms. Serve with a mixed leaf salad for a delicious meal.

INGREDIENTS

10g/¹/₄oz/2 tbsp dried porcini mushrooms
(omit if using wild mushrooms)
20ml/4 tsp olive oil
1 small onion, finely chopped
675g/1¹/₂lb mushrooms, wild or
cultivated, or a combination of both
2 garlic cloves, finely chopped
45ml/3 tbsp chopped fresh parsley
3 tomatoes, skinned and diced
15ml/1 tbsp tomato purée (paste)
175ml/6fl oz/³/₄ cup warm water
1.5ml/¹/₄ tsp fresh thyme leaves, or
1 large pinch of dried thyme
1 bay leaf
350g/12oz/3 cups polenta
salt and ground black pepper
fresh parsley sprigs, to garnish

SERVES 6

1 Soak the dried mushrooms, if using, in a small bowl of warm water for about 20 minutes. Remove the mushrooms with a slotted spoon and rinse them well in several changes of cold water. Set aside. Filter the soaking water through a layer of absorbent kitchen paper placed in a sieve (strainer) and reserve.

2 In a large frying pan, heat the oil and sauté the onion over a low heat until soft and golden.

3 Clean the fresh mushrooms by wiping them with a damp cloth. Cut into slices. When the onion is soft, add the mushrooms to the pan. Stir over a medium to high heat until they give up their liquid. Add the garlic, parsley and diced tomatoes. Cook for 4–5 minutes, stirring occasionally.

4 Soften the tomato purée in the warm water (use only 120ml/4fl oz/¹/₂ cup water if using dried mushrooms). Add the purée to the pan with the herbs. Add the dried mushrooms and soaking liquid, if using, and season with salt and pepper.

5 Reduce the heat to low and cook for 15–20 minutes, stirring occasionally. Remove the pan from the heat and set the sauce aside.

6 Bring 1.5 litres/2¹/₂ pints/6¹/₄ cups water to the boil in a large, heavy pan. Add 15ml/1 tbsp salt.

7 Reduce the heat to a simmer and begin to add the polenta in a fine rain. Stir with a whisk until the polenta has all been incorporated.

8 Switch to a long-handled wooden spoon and continue to stir the polenta over a low to medium heat until it is a thick mass and pulls away from the sides of the pan. This may take 25–50 minutes, depending on the type of polenta used. For best results, never stop stirring the polenta until you remove it from the heat.

9 When the polenta has almost finished cooking, gently reheat the mushroom sauce until piping hot.

10 To serve, spoon the polenta on to a warmed serving platter. Make a well in the centre. Spoon some of the mushroom sauce into the well, and garnish with fresh parsley sprigs.

11 Serve immediately, handing round the remaining mushroom sauce in a separate bowl.

NUTRITIONAL NOTES

Per portion:

Energy	244Kcals/1019kJ
Total fat	3.5g
Saturated fat	0.6g
Cholesterol	0mg
Fibre	1.5g

BAKED CHEESE POLENTA WITH TOMATO SAUCE

Polenta, or cornmeal, is a staple food in Italy. It is cooked in a similar way to porridge, and
eaten soft, or set, cut into shapes, then baked. Serve with crusty Italian bread.

INGREDIENTS

5ml/1 tsp salt
250g/9oz/2¼ cups quick-cook polenta
5ml/1 tsp paprika
2.5ml/½ tsp ground nutmeg
5ml/1 tsp olive oil
1 large onion, finely chopped
2 garlic cloves, crushed
2 x 400g/14oz cans chopped tomatoes
15ml/1 tbsp tomato purée (paste)
5ml/1 tsp sugar
salt and ground black pepper
50g/2oz/½ cup Gruyère cheese, grated

SERVES 6

1 Preheat the oven to 200°C/400°F/Gas 6.
Line a baking tin (pan) (28 × 18cm/11 ×
7in) with clear film (plastic wrap). Bring
1 litre/1¾ pints/4 cups water to the boil
in a pan with the salt.

2 Pour in the polenta in a steady stream and
cook for 5 minutes, stirring continuously.
Beat in the paprika and nutmeg, then
pour the mixture into the prepared tin and
smooth the surface. Leave to cool.

3 Heat the oil in a non-stick pan and
cook the onion and garlic until soft,
stirring occasionally. Stir in the tomatoes,
tomato purée, sugar and seasoning. Bring
to the boil, reduce the heat and simmer
for 20 minutes, stirring occasionally.

NUTRITIONAL NOTES

Per portion:

Energy	219Kcals/918kJ
Total fat	5g
Saturated fat	2g
Cholesterol	0mg
Fibre	1g

4 Turn the cooled polenta out on to a
chopping board, and cut evenly into
5cm/2in squares.

5 Place half the polenta squares in a
greased ovenproof dish. Spoon over half
the tomato sauce, and sprinkle half the
cheese over the top. Repeat the layers.
Bake in the oven for about 25 minutes,
until golden. Serve.

RED PEPPER RISOTTO

This delicious Italian risotto creates a flavourful and low-fat supper or main-course dish,
ideally served with fresh Italian bread.

INGREDIENTS

3 large red (bell) peppers
10ml/2 tsp olive oil
3 large garlic cloves,
thinly sliced
1¹/2 x 400g/14oz cans
chopped tomatoes
2 bay leaves
1.2–1.5 litres/2–2¹/2 pints/5–6¹/4 cups
vegetable stock
450g/1lb/2¹/2 cups arborio rice or
brown rice
6 fresh basil leaves, snipped
salt and ground black pepper

SERVES 4

1 Preheat the grill (broiler). Put the peppers in a grill (broiling) pan and grill (broil) until the skins are blackened and blistered all over. Put the peppers in a bowl, cover with several layers of damp absorbent kitchen paper and leave for 10 minutes. Peel off and discard the skins, then slice the peppers, discarding the cores and seeds. Set aside.

2 Heat the oil in a wide, shallow pan. Add the garlic and tomatoes and cook over a gentle heat for 5 minutes, stirring occasionally, then add the prepared pepper slices and the bay leaves. Stir well and cook gently for 15 minutes.

3 Pour the vegetable stock into a separate large, heavy pan and heat it to simmering point. Stir the rice into the vegetable mixture and cook for about 2 minutes, then add two or three ladlefuls of the hot stock. Cook, stirring occasionally, until all the stock has been absorbed into the rice.

NUTRITIONAL NOTES

Per portion:

Energy	306Kcals/1298kJ
Total fat	3.7g
Saturated fat	0.7g
Cholesterol	0mg
Fibre	2.7g

4 Continue to add stock in this way, making sure each addition has been absorbed before adding the next. When the rice is tender, season with salt and pepper. Remove the pan from the heat, cover and leave to stand for 10 minutes. Remove and discard the bay leaves, then stir in the basil. Serve.

MEDITERRANEAN VEGETABLES WITH CHICKPEAS

—

The flavours of the Mediterranean are captured in this delicious low-fat vegetable dish, ideal for
an appetizer or lunchtime snack, served with fresh crusty bread.

INGREDIENTS
1 onion, sliced
2 leeks, sliced
2 garlic cloves, crushed
1 red (bell) pepper, deseeded and sliced
*1 green (bell) pepper, deseeded
and sliced*
*1 yellow (bell) pepper, deseeded
and sliced*
350g/12oz courgettes (zucchini), sliced
225g/8oz/3 cups mushrooms, sliced
400g/14oz can chopped tomatoes
30ml/2 tbsp ruby port or red wine
30ml/2 tbsp tomato purée (paste)
15ml/1 tbsp tomato ketchup (optional)
400g/14oz can chickpeas
115g/4oz/1 cup pitted black olives
45ml/3 tbsp chopped fresh mixed herbs
salt and ground black pepper
chopped fresh mixed herbs, to garnish

SERVES 6

1 Put the onion, leeks, garlic, red, yellow
and green peppers, courgettes and
mushrooms into a large pan.

COOK'S TIP
For the best Mediterranean flavour, try
to include fresh basil and oregano in the
mixed herbs used in this recipe.

2 Add the tomatoes, port or red wine,
tomato purée and tomato ketchup, if
using, to the pan and mix all the
ingredients together well.

3 Rinse and drain the chickpeas and add
to the pan. Stir to mix.

4 Cover, bring to the boil then reduce the
heat and simmer the mixture gently for
20–30 minutes, until the vegetables are
cooked and tender but not overcooked,
stirring occasionally.

5 Remove the lid of the pan and increase
the heat slightly for the last 10 minutes
of the cooking time, to thicken the sauce,
if you like.

6 Stir in the olives, herbs and seasoning.
Serve either hot or cold, garnished with
chopped mixed herbs.

NUTRITIONAL NOTES
Per portion:

Energy	55Kcals/654kJ
Total fat	4.56g
Saturated fat	0.67g
Cholesterol	0mg
Fibre	6.98g

ROSEMARY ROASTIES

These tasty Italian-style roast potatoes use far less fat than traditional roast potatoes, and because they still have their skins they not only absorb less oil but also have more flavour.

INGREDIENTS
1kg/2¼lb small red potatoes
10ml/2 tsp walnut or sunflower oil
30ml/2 tbsp fresh rosemary leaves
salt and paprika

SERVES 4

1 Preheat the oven to 240°C/475°F/Gas 9. Leave the potatoes whole with the peel on or, if large, cut in half. Place the potatoes in a large pan of cold water and bring to the boil. Drain well.

2 Drizzle the walnut or sunflower oil over the potatoes and shake the pan to coat them evenly.

3 Tip the potatoes into a shallow roasting pan. Sprinkle with rosemary, salt and paprika. Roast in the oven for 30 minutes or until cooked and crisp. Serve hot.

NUTRITIONAL NOTES
Per portion:

Energy	205Kcals/865kJ
Total fat	2.22g
Saturated fat	0.19g
Cholesterol	0mg
Fibre	3.25g

BAKED COURGETTES IN PASSATA

Sliced courgettes, oven-baked with onions, passata and fresh thyme, make a delicious, virtually fat-free vegetable dish.

INGREDIENTS
5ml/1 tsp olive oil
3 large courgettes (zucchini), thinly sliced
½ small red onion, finely chopped
300ml/½ pint/1¼ cups passata
(bottled strained tomatoes)
30ml/2 tbsp chopped fresh thyme
garlic salt and ground black pepper
fresh thyme sprigs, to garnish

SERVES 4

NUTRITIONAL NOTES
Per portion:

Energy	49Kcals/205kJ
Total fat	1.43g
Saturated fat	0.22g
Cholesterol	0mg
Fibre	1.73g

1 Preheat the oven to 190°C/375°F/Gas 5. Brush an ovenproof dish with the olive oil.

2 Arrange half the courgettes and onion in the dish.

3 Spoon half the passata over the vegetables and sprinkle with some of the fresh thyme, then season to taste with garlic salt and pepper.

4 Arrange the remaining courgettes and onion in the dish on top of the passata, then season to taste with more garlic salt and pepper. Spoon over the remaining passata and spread evenly.

5 Cover the dish with foil, then bake in the oven for 40–45 minutes, or until the courgettes are tender. Garnish with sprigs of fresh thyme and serve hot.

FENNEL GRATIN

This is one of the best ways to eat fresh fennel as a snack or vegetable accompaniment.

INGREDIENTS
2 fennel bulbs, about 675g/1¹/2lb total
300ml/¹/2 pint/1¹/4 cups semi-skimmed
(low-fat) milk
15g/¹/2oz/1 tbsp butter
15ml/1 tbsp plain (all-purpose) flour
25g/1oz/scant ¹/2 cup dry
white breadcrumbs
40g/1¹/2oz Gruyère cheese, grated
salt and ground black pepper

SERVES 6

1 Preheat the oven to 240°C/475°F/Gas 9. Discard the stalks and root ends from the fennel. Slice the fennel into quarters and place in a large pan. Pour over the milk, bring to the boil, then simmer for 10–15 minutes until tender.

2 Grease a small baking dish. Remove the fennel pieces with a slotted spoon, reserving the milk. Arrange the fennel pieces in the dish.

3 Melt the butter in a small pan and add the flour. Stir well, then gradually whisk in the reserved milk. Cook the sauce until thickened, stirring.

4 Pour the sauce over the fennel pieces, sprinkle with the breadcrumbs and Gruyère. Season and bake in the oven for about 20 minutes until browned. Serve.

VARIATION
Instead of the Gruyère, Parmesan, Pecorino, mature (sharp) Cheddar or any other strong cheese would work perfectly.

NUTRITIONAL NOTES
Per portion:

Energy	89Kcals/371kJ
Total fat	4.8g
Saturated fat	2.9g
Cholesterol	8.24mg
Fibre	2.5g

ITALIAN SWEET-AND-SOUR ONIONS

Onions are naturally sweet, and when they are cooked at a high temperature the sweetness intensifies. Serve these delicious onions with cooked lean meat or cooked fresh vegetables.

INGREDIENTS
25g/1oz/2 tbsp butter
75ml/5 tbsp sugar
120ml/4fl oz/¹/2 cup white wine vinegar
30ml/2 tbsp balsamic vinegar
675g/1¹/2lb small pickling (pearl)
onions, peeled
salt and ground black pepper

SERVES 6

COOK'S TIP
This recipe also looks delicious when made with either yellow or red onions, cut into slices. Cooking times vary.

1 Melt the butter in a large pan over a gentle heat. Add the sugar and cook until it begins to dissolve, stirring constantly.

2 Add the vinegars to the pan with the onions and heat gently. Season, cover and cook over a moderate heat for 20–25 minutes, stirring occasionally, until the onions are soft when pierced with a knife. Serve hot.

NUTRITIONAL NOTES
Per portion:

Energy	106Kcals/447kJ
Total fat	3.6g
Saturated fat	2.2g
Cholesterol	9.5mg
Fibre	1.3g

COURGETTE AND ASPARAGUS PARCELS

To appreciate the aroma, these Italian-style courgette and asparagus-filled paper parcels should
be broken open at the table. They make a tasty and low-fat vegetable accompaniment.

INGREDIENTS

2 courgettes (zucchini)
1 leek
225g/8oz young asparagus, trimmed
4 tarragon sprigs
4 whole garlic cloves, unpeeled
1 egg, beaten, to glaze
salt and ground black pepper

SERVES 4

1 Preheat the oven to 200°C/400°F/Gas 6.
Using a vegetable peeler, carefully slice
the courgettes lengthways into thin strips.

2 Cut the leek into very fine julienne
strips and cut the asparagus evenly into
5cm/2in lengths.

3 Cut out four sheets of baking parchment
measuring 30 × 38cm/12 × 15in and fold
each one in half. Draw a large curve to
make a heart shape when unfolded. Cut
along the inside of the line and open out.

4 Divide the courgettes, leek and
asparagus evenly between each paper
heart, positioning the filling on one side
of the fold line, then top each portion with
a sprig of tarragon and an unpeeled garlic
clove. Season to taste.

5 Brush the edges of the paper lightly
with the beaten egg and fold over.

6 Twist the edges of the paper together
so that each parcel is completely sealed.
Lay the parcels on a baking sheet.

7 Bake in the preheated oven for 10
minutes. Serve the parcels immediately.

NUTRITIONAL NOTES

Per portion:

Energy	110Kcals/460kJ
Total fat	2.29g
Saturated fat	0.49g
Cholesterol	48mg
Fibre	6.73g

FRENCH BEANS WITH TOMATOES

This is a real Italian summer favourite using the best ripe plum tomatoes and French beans. It is
ideal served as an accompaniment or with fresh Italian bread for a tasty lunch or supper dish.

INGREDIENTS
15ml/1 tbsp olive oil
1 large onion, thinly sliced
2 garlic cloves, finely chopped
6 large ripe plum tomatoes, peeled,
deseeded and coarsely chopped
150ml/¹/4 pint/²/3 cup dry
white wine
450g/1lb French (green) beans, sliced in
half lengthways
16 pitted black olives
10ml/2 tsp lemon juice
salt and ground black pepper

SERVES 4

1 Heat the oil in a large frying pan. Add
the onion and garlic and cook for about
5 minutes until the onion is softened but
not brown, stirring occasionally.

2 Add the chopped tomatoes, white
wine, beans, olives and lemon juice
and cook over a gentle heat for a further
20 minutes, stirring occasionally, until
the sauce is thickened and the beans are
tender. Season with salt and pepper to
taste and serve immediately.

COOK'S TIP
French (green) beans need little
preparation – you simply top and tail
them. When choosing, make sure that
the beans snap easily – this is a sure
sign of freshness.

NUTRITIONAL NOTES
Per portion:

Energy	69Kcals/278kJ
Total fat	2.7g
Saturated fat	0.4g
Cholesterol	0mg
Fibre	2.4g

VARIATION
Any leftovers of this dish are delicious
eaten cold, as a salad, with plenty of
crusty Italian bread to mop up
the juices.

POTATO GNOCCHI

—

Gnocchi are little Italian dumplings made either with mashed potato and flour, as here, or with semolina. They should be light in texture, and must not be overworked while being made.

INGREDIENTS

1kg/2¼lb waxy potatoes, scrubbed
250–300g/9–11oz/2–2½ cups plain
(all-purpose) flour
1 egg
pinch of grated nutmeg
25g/1oz/2 tbsp butter
salt
grated fresh Parmesan cheese, to serve

SERVES 6

1 Place the unpeeled potatoes in a large pan of salted water. Bring to the boil and cook until the potatoes are tender but not falling apart. Drain. Peel as soon as possible, while the potatoes are still hot.

2 On a work surface, spread out a layer of flour. Mash the hot potatoes with a food mill, dropping them on to the flour. Sprinkle with about half of the remaining flour. Mix the flour very lightly into the potatoes.

NUTRITIONAL NOTES

Per portion:

Energy	256Kcals/1083kJ
Total fat	4.6g
Saturated fat	2.4g
Cholesterol	37.8mg
Fibre	2.6g

3 Break the egg into the mixture, add the nutmeg and knead lightly, drawing in more flour as necessary. When the dough is light to the touch and no longer moist or sticky it is ready to be rolled. Do not overwork or the gnocchi will be heavy.

4 Divide the dough into four parts. On a lightly floured board, form each part into a roll about 2cm/³/₄in in diameter, taking care not to overhandle the dough. Cut the rolls crossways into pieces about 2cm/³/₄in long.

5 Hold an ordinary table fork with long tines sideways, leaning on the board. One by one, press and roll the gnocchi lightly along the tines of the fork towards the points, making ridges on one side and a depression from your thumb on the other.

6 Bring a large pan of water to a fast boil. Add salt and drop in about half the gnocchi.

7 When they rise to the surface, after 3–4 minutes, the gnocchi are done. Scoop them out, allow to drain and place in a warmed serving bowl. Dot with butter. Keep warm while the remaining gnocchi are boiling.

8 As soon as they are cooked, toss the drained gnocchi with the butter, sprinkle with a little grated Parmesan, and serve.

VARIATION

Green gnocchi are made in exactly the same way as potato gnocchi, with the addition of fresh or frozen spinach. Use 675g/1½lb fresh spinach, or 400g/14oz frozen leaf spinach. Mix with the potato and the flour in Step 2. Almost any pasta sauce is suitable for serving with gnocchi; they are particularly good with Gorgonzola sauce, or simply drizzled with a little olive oil. Gnocchi can also be served in clear soup.

MEAT AND POULTRY PASTA DISHES

Freshly cooked PASTA *topped or tossed with a tasty* LOW-FAT *sauce made with* MEAT *or poultry and served with crusty Italian* BREAD *or a salad provides an appealing meal for all to* ENJOY. *Choose from a* VARIETY *of low-fat Italian recipes all packed full of* FLAVOUR, *including low-fat versions of classic dishes such as Spaghetti* BOLOGNESE, *Lasagne and Spaghetti alla* CARBONARA.

LASAGNE

—

This is a delicious low-fat version of the classic Italian lasagne, ideal served with a mixed salad and crusty bread for an appetizing supper with friends.

INGREDIENTS

1 large onion, chopped
2 garlic cloves, crushed
500g/1¹/4lb extra-lean minced (ground)
beef or turkey
450g/1lb passata (bottled strained tomatoes)
5ml/1 tsp dried mixed herbs
225g/8oz frozen leaf spinach, defrosted
200g/7oz lasagne verdi
200g/7oz low-fat cottage cheese
mixed salad, to serve

FOR THE SAUCE

25g/1oz low-fat spread
25g/1oz plain (all-purpose) flour
300ml/¹/2 pint/1¹/4 cups skimmed milk
1.5ml/¹/4 tsp ground nutmeg
25g/1oz grated fresh Parmesan cheese
salt and ground black pepper

SERVES 8

1 Put the onion, garlic and minced meat into a non-stick pan. Cook quickly for 5 minutes, stirring with a wooden spoon to separate the pieces, until the meat is lightly browned all over.

COOK'S TIP

Make sure you use the type of lasagne that does not require any pre-cooking for this recipe.

2 Add the passata, herbs and seasoning and stir to mix. Bring to the boil, cover, then reduce the heat and simmer for about 30 minutes, stirring occasionally.

3 Make the sauce: put all the sauce ingredients, except the Parmesan cheese, into a pan. Cook until the sauce thickens, whisking continuously until bubbling and smooth. Turn the heat off. Adjust the seasoning to taste, add the Parmesan cheese to the sauce and stir to mix.

NUTRITIONAL NOTES

Per portion:

Energy	244Kcals/1032kJ
Total fat	4.8g
Saturated fat	1.9g
Cholesterol	37.9mg
Fibre	2g

4 Preheat the oven to 190°C/375°F/Gas 5. Lay the spinach leaves out on sheets of absorbent kitchen paper and pat them until they are dry.

5 Layer the meat mixture, lasagne, cottage cheese and spinach leaves in a 2 litre/3¹/2 pint/8 cup ovenproof dish, starting and ending with a layer of meat.

6 Spoon the sauce over the top to cover the meat completely and bake in the oven for 40–50 minutes or until bubbling. Serve with a mixed salad.

TAGLIATELLE WITH MEAT SAUCE

This recipe is an authentic meat sauce – ragù – from the city of Bologna in Emilia-Romagna. It is quite rich and very delicious, and is always served with tagliatelle, never with spaghetti.

INGREDIENTS
450g/1lb dried tagliatelle
salt and ground black pepper
grated fresh Parmesan cheese,
to serve (optional)

FOR THE BOLOGNESE MEAT SAUCE
1 onion
2 carrots
2 celery sticks
2 garlic cloves
15ml/1 tbsp olive oil
115g/4oz lean back bacon, diced
250g/9oz extra-lean minced (ground) beef
250g/9oz extra-lean minced (ground) pork
120ml/4fl oz/1/2 cup dry white wine
2 × 400g/14oz cans crushed
Italian plum tomatoes
475–750ml/16fl oz–1 1/4 pints/2–3 cups
beef stock

SERVES 8

1 Make the meat sauce. Chop all the fresh vegetables finely. Heat the oil in a large frying pan or pan. Add the chopped vegetables and the bacon and cook over a medium heat, stirring frequently, for 10 minutes or until the vegetables have softened.

2 Add the minced beef and pork, reduce the heat and cook gently for 10 minutes, stirring frequently and breaking up any lumps in the meat with a wooden spoon.

3 Stir in salt and pepper to taste, then add the wine and stir again. Simmer for about 5 minutes, or until reduced.

4 Add the tomatoes and 250ml/8fl oz/ 1 cup of the stock and bring to the boil. Stir the sauce well, then reduce the heat. Half cover the pan with a lid and leave to simmer very gently for 2 hours. Stir occasionally and add more stock as it becomes absorbed.

5 Simmer the sauce, without a lid, for a further 30 minutes, stirring frequently. Meanwhile, cook the pasta in a large pan of boiling salted water, according to the packet instructions, until tender or al dente. Taste the sauce and adjust the seasoning. Drain the cooked pasta and tip it into a warmed bowl. Pour the meat sauce over the pasta and toss well. Serve immediately, sprinkled with grated Parmesan, if using.

NUTRITIONAL NOTES
Per portion:

Energy	185Kcals/782kJ
Total fat	5g
Saturated fat	1.7g
Cholesterol	36.3mg
Fibre	1.8g

LAMB AND SWEET PEPPER SAUCE

—

This simple sauce is a speciality of the Abruzzo-Molise region of Italy, east of Rome, where it is traditionally served with *maccheroni alla chitarra* – square-shaped long macaroni.

2 Sprinkle in the garlic and add the bay leaves, then pour in the wine and let it bubble until reduced.

3 Add the tomatoes and peppers and stir to mix. Season again. Cover with the lid, bring to the boil, then reduce the heat and simmer gently for 45–55 minutes or until the lamb is very tender. Stir occasionally during cooking and add a little water if the sauce becomes too dry. Meanwhile, cook the pasta in a large pan of boiling salted water, according to the packet instructions, until tender or al dente. Drain well. Remove and discard the bay leaves from the lamb sauce before serving it with the cooked pasta.

INGREDIENTS
15ml/1 tbsp olive oil
250g/9oz boneless lean lamb neck fillet, diced quite small
2 garlic cloves, finely chopped
2 bay leaves, torn
250ml/8fl oz/1 cup dry white wine
4 ripe Italian plum tomatoes, skinned and chopped
2 red (bell) peppers, deseeded and diced
450g/1lb dried spaghetti
salt and ground black pepper

SERVES 6

1 Heat the oil in a medium frying pan or pan, add the lamb and a little salt and pepper. Cook over a medium to high heat for about 10 minutes, stirring frequently, until browned all over.

NUTRITIONAL NOTES
Per portion:

Energy	179Kcals/755kJ
Total fat	5g
Saturated fat	1.8g
Cholesterol	28mg
Fibre	1.4g

COOK'S TIP
You can make your own fresh *maccheroni alla chitarra* or buy the dried pasta from an Italian delicatessen. Alternatively, this sauce is just as good served with ordinary spaghetti or long or short macaroni.

VARIATION
The peppers don't have to be red. Use yellow, orange or green if you prefer; either one colour or a mixture.

TAGLIATELLE WITH MILANESE SAUCE

Tagliatelle is served with a tasty, low-fat version of the classic Milanese sauce to create this
flavourful dish, ideal for a family meal.

INGREDIENTS

1 onion, finely chopped
1 celery stick, finely chopped
*1 red (bell) pepper, deseeded
and diced*
1–2 garlic cloves, crushed
*150ml/¼ pint/⅔ cup vegetable
or chicken stock*
400g/14oz can tomatoes
15ml/1 tbsp tomato purée (paste)
10ml/2 tsp caster (superfine) sugar
*5ml/1 tsp dried
mixed herbs*
350g/12oz tagliatelle
*115g/4oz button (white) or small cap
mushrooms, sliced*
60ml/4 tbsp dry white wine
*115g/4oz lean cooked ham,
coarsely diced*
salt and ground black pepper
*15ml/1 tbsp chopped fresh parsley,
to garnish*

SERVES 4

1 Put the onion, celery, red pepper and
garlic into a pan.

2 Add the stock, bring to the boil and
cook for 5 minutes or until tender,
stirring occasionally.

3 Add the tomatoes, tomato purée,
sugar and dried herbs. Season with salt
and pepper.

4 Bring to the boil then reduce the heat
and simmer for 30 minutes, stirring
occasionally, until the sauce is thick.

5 Cook the pasta in a large pan of boiling
salted water, according to the packet
instructions, until tender or al dente.
Drain thoroughly.

6 Meanwhile, put the mushrooms into
a small pan with the white wine, cover
and cook for 3–4 minutes until the
mushrooms are tender and all the wine
has been absorbed, stirring occasionally.

7 Stir the mushrooms and ham into the
tomato sauce and reheat gently over a low
heat until piping hot.

8 Transfer the pasta to a warmed serving
dish and spoon the sauce on top. Garnish
with chopped parsley and serve.

NUTRITIONAL NOTES

Per portion:

Energy	405Kcals/1700kJ
Total fat	3.5g
Saturated fat	0.8g
Cholesterol	17mg
Fibre	4.5g

COOK'S TIP
To reduce the calorie and fat content
even more, omit the ham and use
corn kernels or cooked broccoli
florets instead.

SPAGHETTI ALLA CARBONARA

This is a low-fat variation of the classic Italian charcoal burner's spaghetti, using lean smoked back bacon and low-fat cream cheese. Serve with a few Parmesan cheese shavings.

2 Add the wine and boil rapidly until reduced by half. Whisk in the cheese and season to taste with salt and pepper.

3 Meanwhile, cook the spaghetti in a large pan of boiling, salted water for 10–12 minutes, until tender or al dente. Drain thoroughly.

4 Return the cooked spaghetti to the pan with the sauce and parsley, toss well and serve immediately topped with a few thin shavings of Parmesan cheese.

INGREDIENTS

150g/5oz lean smoked back bacon
rashers (strips)
1 onion, chopped
1–2 garlic cloves, crushed
150ml/¼ pint/⅔ cup chicken stock
150ml/¼ pint/⅔ cup dry white wine
200g/7oz low-fat soft cheese
450g/1lb chilli and garlic-flavoured
dried spaghetti
30ml/2 tbsp chopped fresh parsley
salt and ground black pepper
15g/½oz shaved fresh
Parmesan cheese, to serve

SERVES 4

1 Cut the bacon rashers into 1cm/½in strips. Fry quickly in a non-stick frying pan for 2–3 minutes, stirring. Add the onion, garlic and stock to the pan. Bring to the boil, cover, then reduce the heat and simmer for about 5 minutes until tender.

NUTRITIONAL NOTES

Per portion:

Energy	428Kcals/1815kJ
Total fat	4.6g
Saturated fat	1.6g
Cholesterol	9.96mg
Fibre	3g

PAPPARDELLE WITH RABBIT SAUCE

—

This delicious low-fat pasta dish comes from the north of Italy, where rabbit sauces for pasta
are very popular. Serve with crusty fresh bread and a mixed leaf salad for a filling meal.

INGREDIENTS

15g/¹/₂oz/¹/₄ cup dried porcini mushrooms
175ml/6fl oz/³/₄ cup warm water
1 small onion
¹/₂ carrot
¹/₂ celery stick
2 bay leaves
15ml/1 tbsp olive oil
40g/1¹/₂oz lean back bacon, chopped
15ml/1 tbsp roughly chopped fresh flat leaf
parsley, plus extra to garnish
350g/12oz boneless lean rabbit meat
90ml/6 tbsp dry white wine
200g/7oz can chopped Italian plum
tomatoes or 200ml/7fl oz/scant 1 cup
passata (bottled strained tomatoes)
450g/1lb dried pappardelle
salt and ground black pepper

SERVES 6

1 Put the dried mushrooms in a bowl,
pour over the warm water and leave to
soak for 15–20 minutes. Finely chop the
fresh vegetables. Make a tear in each bay
leaf, so they release their flavour.

2 Heat the oil in a frying pan or medium
pan. Add the vegetables, bacon and
parsley and cook for about 5 minutes,
stirring occasionally.

NUTRITIONAL NOTES

Per portion:

Energy	166Kcals/699kJ
Total fat	4.7g
Saturated fat	1.4g
Cholesterol	33.9mg
Fibre	1.4g

3 Add the pieces of rabbit and fry on both
sides for 3–4 minutes, stirring frequently.
Pour the wine over and let it bubble
and reduce for a few minutes, then
add the tomatoes or passata. Drain the
mushrooms and pour the soaking liquid
into the pan. Chop the mushrooms and
add them to the pan with the bay leaves
and salt and pepper to taste. Stir well,
cover, bring to the boil, then reduce the
heat and simmer for 35–40 minutes until
the rabbit is tender, stirring occasionally.

4 Remove from the heat and lift out the
rabbit with a slotted spoon. Cut into bite-
size chunks and stir into the sauce.
Remove the bay leaves. Add more salt
and pepper, if needed. Cook the pasta in
a large pan of boiling salted water,
according to the packet instructions,
until tender or al dente. Meanwhile,
reheat the sauce until piping hot. Drain
the pasta and toss with the sauce in a
warmed bowl. Serve immediately,
sprinkled with parsley.

FISH AND SHELLFISH PASTA DISHES

The wide variety of different SHAPES, *sizes and* FLAVOURS *of fresh and dried pasta creates a wonderful basis for many delicious and* NUTRITIOUS *low-fat Italian fish and shellfish* PASTA *dishes. We include a tempting selection of no-fuss recipes, using a variety of* FISH *and* SHELLFISH, *to please every palate. Choose from Farfalle with* TUNA, *Smoked Trout Cannelloni, Tagliatelle with Scallops or Vermicelli with* CLAM *Sauce.*

FUSILLI WITH SMOKED TROUT

Fusilli pasta is served with a delicious smoked trout and vegetable sauce to create a flavourful lunch or supper dish. Smoked salmon may be used in place of the trout, for a tasty change.

INGREDIENTS

2 carrots, cut into julienne sticks
1 leek, cut into julienne sticks
2 celery sticks, cut into julienne sticks
150ml/¼ pint/⅔ cup vegetable or fish stock
225g/8oz smoked trout fillets, skinned and cut into strips
200g/7oz low-fat soft cheese
150ml/¼ pint/⅔ cup medium sweet white wine or fish stock
15ml/1 tbsp chopped fresh dill or fennel
225g/8oz dried fusilli lunghi
salt and ground black pepper
fresh dill sprigs, to garnish

SERVES 6

1 Put the carrots, leek and celery into a pan with the vegetable or fish stock. Bring to the boil and cook quickly for 4–5 minutes until the vegetables are tender and most of the stock has evaporated, stirring occasionally. Turn the heat off and stir in the smoked trout. Set aside.

2 To make the sauce, put the soft cheese and wine or fish stock into a pan and cook, whisking until smooth. Season. Stir in the dill or fennel.

3 Meanwhile, cook the pasta in a large pan of boiling salted water according to the instructions, until tender or al dente. Drain thoroughly. Return to the pan, add the sauce, toss and transfer to a serving bowl. Top with the vegetables and trout. Serve garnished with dill sprigs.

NUTRITIONAL NOTES
Per portion:

Energy	234Kcals/989kJ
Total fat	3.7g
Saturated fat	1.3g
Cholesterol	40mg
Fibre	1.7g

PASTA WITH TOMATO AND TUNA

—

Pasta shells are topped with a tasty tuna and tomato sauce to create this delicious,
low-fat Italian-style pasta dish.

3 Meanwhile, cook the pasta in a large
pan of boiling, salted water according to
the packet instructions, until tender or al
dente. Drain thoroughly and transfer to a
warm serving dish.

INGREDIENTS
1 onion, finely chopped
1 celery stick, finely chopped
1 red (bell) pepper, deseeded and diced
1 garlic clove, crushed
150ml/1/4 pint/2/3 cup chicken stock
400g/14oz can chopped tomatoes
15ml/1 tbsp tomato purée (paste)
10ml/2 tsp caster (superfine) sugar
15ml/1 tbsp chopped fresh basil
15ml/1 tbsp chopped fresh parsley
450g/1lb/4 cups dried conchiglie
400g/14oz can tuna in brine, drained
30ml/2 tbsp capers in vinegar, drained
salt and ground black pepper

SERVES 6

1 Put the onion, celery, red pepper and
garlic into a pan. Add the stock, bring to
the boil and cook for 5 minutes until the
stock has reduced significantly.

2 Add the tomatoes, tomato purée, sugar
and herbs. Season to taste with salt and
pepper and bring to the boil. Reduce the
heat and simmer for about 30 minutes
until thick, stirring occasionally.

4 Flake the tuna into large chunks and
add to the sauce with the capers. Cook
gently for 1–2 minutes, stirring, then
pour over the pasta, toss gently and
serve immediately.

VARIATION
If fresh herbs are not available, use a
400g/14oz can of chopped tomatoes
with herbs and add 5–10ml/1–2 tsp
dried mixed herbs, in place of the
fresh herbs.

NUTRITIONAL NOTES
Per portion:

Energy	369Kcals/1549kJ
Total fat	2.1g
Saturated fat	0.4g
Cholesterol	34mg
Fibre	4g

SAFFRON PAPPARDELLE

—

Serve this flavourful and low-fat Italian pasta dish with a mixed green salad and fresh Italian
bread for a wholesome and nutritious meal.

INGREDIENTS

large pinch of saffron threads
4 sun-dried tomatoes, chopped
5ml/1 tsp chopped fresh thyme
12 large fresh whole prawns (shrimp)
in their shells
225g/8oz baby squid
225g/8oz skinless monkfish fillet
2–3 garlic cloves, crushed
2 small onions, quartered
1 small bulb fennel, trimmed and sliced
150ml/¹/4 pint/²/3 cup white wine
225g/8oz dried pappardelle
salt and ground black pepper
30ml/2 tbsp chopped fresh parsley,
to garnish

SERVES 4

1 Put the saffron, sun-dried tomatoes and
thyme into a bowl with 60ml/4 tbsp hot
water. Leave to soak for 30 minutes.

COOK'S TIP

Make sure you use the sun-dried
tomatoes for soaking in Step 1, rather
than the ones preserved in oil. Do not
try to substitute turmeric for the
saffron in this recipe; although the
colour will be similar, the flavour
will be quite different.

2 Wash the prawns and carefully remove
and discard the shells, but leave the
heads and tails intact. Pull the head from
the body of each squid and remove and
discard the quill. Cut the tentacles from
the head and rinse under cold water. Pull
off and discard the outer skin and cut the
flesh into 5mm/¹/4in rings. Cut the
monkfish into 2.5cm/1in cubes. Set aside.

3 Put the garlic, onions and fennel into a
pan with the wine. Cover and simmer for
5 minutes until tender. Stir occasionally.

NUTRITIONAL NOTES
Per portion:

Energy	381Kcals/1602kJ
Total fat	3.5g
Saturated fat	0.6g
Cholesterol	34mg
Fibre	3.2g

4 Stir in the monkfish and the saffron
mixture. Cover and cook for 3 minutes,
then stir in the prawns and squid. Cover
and cook gently for 1–2 minutes (do not
overcook). Season to taste.

5 Meanwhile, cook the pasta in a large
pan of boiling, salted water according to
the packet instructions, until tender or
al dente. Drain thoroughly.

6 Divide the pasta among four serving
dishes and top with the sauce. Sprinkle
with parsley and serve immediately.

FARFALLE WITH TUNA

—

This is a quick and simple dish that makes a good low-fat weekday supper if you have canned
tomatoes and tuna in the store cupboard. Serve with crusty fresh Italian bread.

4 Meanwhile, cook the pasta in a large
pan of boiling salted water according to
the packet instructions, until tender
or al dente.

5 Drain the tuna and flake it with a fork.
Add to the sauce with about 60ml/4 tbsp
of the pasta water and stir to mix. Adjust
the seasoning to taste.

6 Drain the pasta well and tip it into a
warmed serving bowl. Pour the sauce
over the top and toss to mix. Serve
immediately, garnished with oregano.

INGREDIENTS

15ml/1 tbsp olive oil
1 small onion, finely chopped
1 garlic clove, finely chopped
400g/14oz can chopped Italian
plum tomatoes
45ml/3 tbsp dry white wine
8–10 pitted black olives, sliced into rings
10ml/2 tsp chopped fresh oregano or
5ml/1 tsp dried oregano, plus extra fresh
oregano, to garnish
350g/12oz/3 cups dried farfalle
175g/6oz can tuna in brine
salt and ground black pepper

SERVES 4

1 Heat the olive oil in a medium frying
pan or pan, and add the chopped onion
and garlic.

2 Cook gently for 2–3 minutes until
the onion is soft and golden, stirring
occasionally.

3 Add the tomatoes and bring to the boil,
then add the white wine and simmer for a
minute or so. Stir in the olives and
oregano, with salt and pepper to taste,
then cover and cook for 20–25 minutes,
stirring occasionally.

NUTRITIONAL NOTES

Per portion:

Energy	387Kcals/1643kJ
Total fat	4.9g
Saturated fat	0.8g
Cholesterol	21.3mg
Fibre	3.5g

MACARONI WITH BROCCOLI AND CAULIFLOWER

This is a typical southern Italian dish, full of flavour and low in fat too. Without the anchovies,
it can be served to vegetarians.

INGREDIENTS

175g/6oz cauliflower florets, cut into
small sprigs
175g/6oz broccoli florets, cut into
small sprigs
350g/12oz/3 cups dried
short-cut macaroni
15ml/1 tbsp extra virgin olive oil
1 onion, finely chopped
30ml/2 tbsp pine nuts (optional)
1 sachet of saffron powder, dissolved in
15ml/1 tbsp warm water
15ml/1 tbsp raisins
30ml/2 tbsp sun-dried tomato
purée (paste)
4 bottled or canned anchovies in olive oil,
drained and chopped
salt and ground black pepper
grated fresh Pecorino cheese, to serve

SERVES 4

3 Meanwhile, heat the olive oil in a large
frying pan or pan, add the onion and cook
over a low to medium heat, stirring
frequently, for 2–3 minutes or until
golden. Add the pine nuts, if using, the
broccoli and cauliflower, and the saffron
water. Add the raisins, sun-dried tomato
purée and a couple of ladlefuls of the
pasta cooking water until the mixture has
the consistency of a sauce. Finally, add
plenty of pepper.

4 Stir well, cook for 1–2 minutes, then
add the chopped anchovies. Drain the
pasta and tip it into the vegetable
mixture. Toss well, then taste for
seasoning and add salt if necessary.
Serve the pasta immediately in four
warmed bowls, sprinkled with freshly
grated Pecorino.

NUTRITIONAL NOTES

Per portion:

Energy	339Kcals/1438kJ
Total fat	5g
Saturated fat	0.7g
Cholesterol	0mg
Fibre	4.5g

1 Cook the cauliflower in a large pan of
boiling salted water for 3 minutes.
Add the broccoli and boil for a further
2 minutes. Remove the vegetables from
the pan with a large slotted spoon, place
on a plate and set aside.

2 Add the pasta to the vegetable cooking
water and bring back to the boil. Cook
the pasta according to the packet
instructions, until it is tender or al dente.

SMOKED TROUT CANNELLONI

Cannelloni are stuffed with a tasty smoked trout filling, topped with a low-fat cheese sauce and
oven-baked to create this appetizing Italian lunch or supper dish.

INGREDIENTS

1 large onion, finely chopped
1 garlic clove, crushed
60ml/4 tbsp vegetable stock
2 × 400g/14oz cans chopped tomatoes
2.5ml/¹/2 tsp dried mixed herbs
1 smoked trout, weighing about 400g/14oz
75g/3oz/³/4 cup frozen peas, thawed
75g/3oz/1¹/2 cups fresh breadcrumbs
16 cannelloni tubes
salt and ground black pepper
mixed salad, to serve

FOR THE CHEESE SAUCE

25g/1oz/2 tbsp low-fat spread
25g/1oz/¹/4 cup plain (all-purpose) flour
350ml/12fl oz/1¹/2 cups skimmed milk
freshly grated nutmeg
15g/¹/2oz/1¹/2 tbsp finely grated fresh
Parmesan cheese

SERVES 6

1 Simmer the onion, garlic and stock in a
large covered pan for 3 minutes. Uncover
and continue to cook, stirring
occasionally, until reduced entirely.

COOK'S TIP

Smoked trout can be bought already
filleted or whole. If you buy fillets,
you'll need 225g/8oz fish.

2 Stir in the tomatoes and herbs. Simmer
uncovered for a further 10 minutes, or
until very thick, stirring occasionally.

3 Meanwhile, skin the smoked trout with
a sharp knife. Carefully flake the flesh
and discard all the bones. Mix with the
tomato mixture, peas, breadcrumbs, salt
and pepper in a large bowl.

4 Preheat the oven to 190°C/375°F/Gas 5.
Spoon the filling into the cannelloni
tubes and arrange in an ovenproof dish.
Set aside.

5 Make the sauce. Put the low-fat spread,
flour and milk into a pan and cook over a
medium heat, whisking until the sauce
thickens. Simmer for 2–3 minutes,
stirring continuously. Season to taste
with salt, pepper and nutmeg.

6 Pour the sauce over the cannelloni and
sprinkle with the Parmesan cheese. Bake
in the oven for 35–40 minutes, or until
the top is golden brown. Serve with a
mixed salad.

NUTRITIONAL NOTES

Per portion:

Energy	306Kcals/1298kJ
Total fat	5g
Saturated fat	1.3g
Cholesterol	45.8mg
Fibre	3g

TAGLIATELLE WITH SCALLOPS

—

Scallops and brandy add a taste of luxury to this appetizing pasta sauce, ideal as a supper dish.

INGREDIENTS
200g/7oz scallops, sliced
30ml/2 tbsp plain (all-purpose) flour
15ml/1 tbsp olive oil
2 spring onions (scallions),
cut into thin rings
1/2–1 small fresh red chilli, deseeded
and very finely chopped
30ml/2 tbsp finely chopped fresh flat
leaf parsley
60ml/4 tbsp brandy
105ml/7 tbsp fish stock
275g/10oz fresh spinach-
flavoured tagliatelle
salt and ground black pepper

SERVES 4

1 Toss the scallops in the flour, shaking the excess. Bring a large pan of salted water to the boil for the pasta. Meanwhile, heat the oil in a frying pan. Add the spring onions, chilli and half the parsley and cook, stirring frequently, for 1–2 minutes over a medium heat. Add the scallops and toss for 1–2 minutes.

2 Pour the brandy over the scallops, then set it alight. When the flames have died down, pour in the stock, season and stir. Simmer for 2–3 minutes, then cover and remove from the heat. Cook the pasta according to the packet instructions. Drain, add to the sauce and toss over a medium heat until mixed. Serve immediately.

NUTRITIONAL NOTES
Per portion:

Energy	372Kcals/1576kJ
Total fat	4.8g
Saturated fat	0.7g
Cholesterol	0.0mg
Fibre	2.2g

SPAGHETTI WITH SQUID AND PEAS

—

In Tuscany, squid is often cooked with peas in a tomato sauce. This low-fat recipe is a tasty variation on the theme, and it works very well.

INGREDIENTS
450g/1lb prepared squid
10ml/2 tsp olive oil
1 small onion, finely chopped
400g/14oz can chopped Italian
plum tomatoes
1 garlic clove, finely chopped
15ml/1 tbsp red wine vinegar
5ml/1 tsp sugar
10ml/2 tsp finely chopped fresh rosemary
115g/4oz/1 cup frozen peas
275g/10oz dried spaghetti
15ml/1 tbsp chopped fresh flat leaf parsley
salt and ground black pepper

SERVES 4

1 Cut the prepared squid into strips about 5mm/¼in wide. Finely chop any tentacles. Set aside. Heat the oil in a frying pan, add the onion and cook gently, stirring, for about 5 minutes until softened. Add the squid, tomatoes, garlic, vinegar and sugar and stir to mix.

NUTRITIONAL NOTES
Per portion:

Energy	285Kcals/1206kJ
Total fat	4g
Saturated fat	0.4g
Cholesterol	0.0mg
Fibre	3g

2 Add the rosemary and seasoning. Bring to the boil, stirring, then cover, reduce the heat, and simmer for 20 minutes, stirring occasionally. Stir in the peas and cook for a further 10 minutes. Cook the pasta according to the packet instructions. Serve with the sauce and the parsley.

HOT SPICY PRAWNS WITH CAMPANELLE

—

**This low-fat prawn sauce tossed with hot pasta creates an ideal Italian-style suppertime dish.
Add less or more chilli depending on how hot you like your food.**

INGREDIENTS

*225g/8oz cooked, peeled
tiger prawns (shrimp)
1–2 garlic cloves, crushed
finely grated rind of 1 lemon
15ml/1 tbsp fresh lemon juice
1.5ml/¼ tsp red chilli paste or 1 large
pinch of chilli powder
15ml/1 tbsp light soy sauce
150g/5oz lean smoked back
bacon rashers (strips)
1 shallot or small onion,
finely chopped
60ml/4 tbsp dry white wine
225g/8oz/2 cups dried campanelle or
other dried pasta shapes
60ml/4 tbsp fish stock
4 firm ripe tomatoes, peeled,
deseeded and chopped
30ml/2 tbsp chopped
fresh parsley
salt and ground black pepper*

SERVES 4

1 In a glass bowl, mix the prawns with the garlic, lemon rind and juice, then stir in the chilli paste or powder and soy sauce.

2 Season with salt and pepper, then cover and leave to marinate in a cool place for at least 1 hour.

3 Grill (broil) the bacon rashers under a hot grill (broiler) until cooked, then cut them into 5mm/¼in dice. Set aside.

4 Put the shallot or onion and white wine into a pan, bring to the boil, cover and cook for 2–3 minutes or until it is tender and the wine has reduced by half. Set aside.

5 Meanwhile, cook the pasta in a large pan of boiling salted water according to the packet instructions, until tender or al dente. Drain thoroughly and keep hot.

COOK'S TIP

To save time later, the prawns (shrimp) and marinade ingredients can be mixed together, covered and chilled in the refrigerator overnight, until ready to use.

6 Just before serving, put the prawns with their marinade into a large frying pan, bring to the boil quickly and add the cooked bacon and fish stock. Heat through for 1 minute, stirring.

7 Add to the hot pasta with the shallot or onion mixture, chopped tomatoes and parsley. Toss quickly to mix and serve immediately.

NUTRITIONAL NOTES

Per portion:

Energy	214Kcals/908kJ
Total fat	3g
Saturated fat	0.9g
Cholesterol	37.5mg
Fibre	1.4g

VEGETARIAN
PASTA
DISHES

This appetizing MEDLEY *of vegetarian pasta dishes brings together a wealth of* DELICIOUS *ingredients to create a collection of low-fat recipes* PACKED *with goodness and the flavours of Italy for family and friends to* RELISH. *Select from recipes such as Tagliatelle with Sun-Dried* TOMATOES, *Mushroom Bolognese, Penne with Artichokes or* TAGLIATELLE *with Hazelnut Pesto.*

CONCHIGLIE WITH TOMATOES AND ROCKET

—

Cooked pasta shells, tossed together with lightly cooked tomatoes and fresh rocket, makes a
tasty low-fat dish that is ideal for a summer lunch or supper.

INGREDIENTS

450g/1lb/4 cups dried conchiglie
450g/1lb ripe cherry tomatoes
75g/3oz fresh rocket (arugula)
15ml/1 tbsp extra virgin olive oil
15g/¹/₂oz fresh Parmesan cheese
salt and ground black pepper

SERVES 4

1 Cook the pasta in a large pan of boiling
salted water, according to the packet
instructions, until tender or al dente.
Stir occasionally.

2 While the pasta is cooking, halve the
cherry tomatoes. Trim, wash and dry
the rocket.

3 Heat the oil in a large pan, add the
halved tomatoes and cook for barely
1 minute. The tomatoes should only just
heat through and not disintegrate.

4 Meanwhile, cut the Parmesan cheese
into fine shavings, using a swivel
vegetable peeler.

COOK'S TIP

This pasta dish relies for its success
on a salad green called rocket
(arugula). Available in most large
supermarkets, it is a leaf that is easily
grown in the garden or a window-box
and tastes slightly peppery. When you
buy rocket, make sure the leaves are
very fresh with no sign of wilting.
Rocket does not keep well unless it has
been pre-packaged. To keep it for a
day or two, wrap it in damp kitchen
paper and store in the refrigerator.

5 Drain the pasta and tip it into the pan
with the tomatoes.

6 Add the rocket and then carefully
stir to mix and heat through. Season
well with salt and pepper and serve
immediately, topped with a little shaved
Parmesan cheese.

VARIATIONS

• You might like to try adding
1.5ml/¹/₄ tsp dried chilli flakes and
2 finely chopped garlic cloves to
this dish. Simply add them to the oil
and fry gently for a minute or so
before adding the tomatoes.
• Use a different type of pasta such
as fusilli in place of the conchiglie.
• In place of the rocket, try
fresh watercress.

NUTRITIONAL NOTES
Per portion:

Energy	329Kcals/1396kJ
Total fat	5g
Saturated fat	1.2g
Cholesterol	2.3mg
Fibre	3.5g

MUSHROOM BOLOGNESE

A quick – and exceedingly tasty – vegetarian version of the classic Italian dish. This dish is easy
to prepare and makes a very satisfying low-fat meal.

INGREDIENTS
450g/1lb mushrooms
15ml/1 tbsp olive oil
1 onion, chopped
1 garlic clove, crushed
15ml/1 tbsp tomato purée (paste)
400g/14oz can chopped tomatoes
45ml/3 tbsp chopped fresh oregano
*450g/1lb fresh pasta, such as spaghetti
or tagliatelle*
salt and ground black pepper
*15g/¹/₂oz shaved fresh Parmesan cheese,
to serve (optional)*

SERVES 4

3 Add the prepared mushrooms to the
pan and mix them gently with the olive
oil and crushed garlic. Cook over a high
heat for about 3–4 minutes, stirring the
mixture occasionally.

5 Meanwhile, bring a large pan of
salted water to the boil. Cook the pasta
in the boiling water for 2–3 minutes, or
according to the packet instructions,
until tender or al dente.

1 Trim the mushroom stems neatly, then
cut each mushroom into quarters. Set
them aside.

4 Stir in the tomato purée, chopped
tomatoes and 15ml/1 tbsp of the oregano.
Cover, reduce the heat, then cook for
about 5 minutes, stirring occasionally.

6 Season the mushroom Bolognese sauce
with salt and pepper. Drain the pasta,
turn it into a bowl and add the mushroom
mixture. Toss to mix well. Serve in
individual bowls, topped with shavings
of fresh Parmesan, if using, and the
remaining chopped fresh oregano.

2 Heat the olive oil in a large pan. Add
the onion and garlic and cook them for
2–3 minutes, stirring occasionally.

COOK'S TIP
If you prefer to use dried pasta, make
this the first thing that you cook. It will
take 10–12 minutes to cook, during
which time you can make the
mushroom mixture. Use 350g/12oz
dried pasta.

NUTRITIONAL NOTES
Per portion:

Energy	404Kcals/1717kJ
Total fat	4.9g
Saturated fat	0.6g
Cholesterol	0mg
Fibre	5g

TAGLIATELLE WITH SPINACH GNOCCHI

Italian-style gnocchi are extremely smooth and light and make a delicious accompaniment to this
flavourful low-fat pasta dish.

INGREDIENTS

450g/1lb mixed flavoured fresh tagliatelle
15g/¹/₂oz shaved fresh Parmesan cheese,
to garnish (optional)

FOR THE SPINACH GNOCCHI

450g/1lb frozen chopped spinach
1 small onion, finely chopped
1 garlic clove, crushed
1.5ml/¹/₄ tsp ground nutmeg
400g/14oz low-fat cottage cheese
115g/4oz dried white breadcrumbs
75g/3oz semolina or plain
(all-purpose) flour
50g/2oz grated fresh Parmesan cheese
3 egg whites

FOR THE TOMATO SAUCE

1 onion, finely chopped
1 celery stick, finely chopped
1 red (bell) pepper, deseeded and diced
1 garlic clove, crushed
150ml/¹/₄ pint/²/₃ cup vegetable stock
400g/14oz can tomatoes
15ml/1 tbsp tomato purée (paste)
10ml/2 tsp caster (superfine) sugar
5ml/1 tsp dried oregano
salt and ground black pepper

SERVES 6

1 To make the tomato sauce, put the
onion, celery, pepper and garlic into a
non-stick pan. Add the stock, bring to the
boil and cook for 5 minutes or until
tender, stirring occasionally.

2 Stir in the tomatoes, tomato purée,
sugar and oregano. Season to taste, bring
to the boil, then reduce the heat and
simmer for 30 minutes until thick, stirring
occasionally. Keep hot.

3 Meanwhile, make the gnocchi. Put the
spinach, onion and garlic into a pan,
cover and cook until the spinach is
defrosted. Remove the lid for a minute or
so, and increase the heat. Cook until the
liquid has evaporated. Season with salt,
pepper and nutmeg. Turn into a bowl and
leave to cool. Mix in the remaining
gnocchi ingredients. Shape into about
30 ovals and refrigerate for 30 minutes.

4 Cook the spinach gnocchi in a large
pan of boiling salted water for about
5 minutes. Remove with a slotted spoon
and drain. Keep hot. Meanwhile, cook
the tagliatelle in a large pan of boiling
salted water, according to the packet
instructions, until tender or al dente.
Drain well. Transfer the pasta to serving
plates, top with the gnocchi, the tomato
sauce and shavings of Parmesan cheese,
if using. Serve immediately.

NUTRITIONAL NOTES

Per portion:

Energy	189Kcals/803kJ
Total fat	2g
Saturated fat	0.8g
Cholesterol	3.3mg
Fibre	2.9g

RATATOUILLE PENNE BAKE

—

Mixed Mediterranean vegetables and penne are tossed together and grilled until lightly
toasted to create this delicious and low-fat pasta meal.

3 Put the aubergine, courgettes, pepper,
onion and remaining garlic into a pan,
with the stock. Bring to the boil, cover
and cook for about 10 minutes until
tender, stirring occasionally. Remove
the lid and boil until all the stock
has evaporated. Add the prepared
tomatoes and herbs and cook for a
further 3 minutes, stirring occasionally.
Season to taste with salt and pepper.

INGREDIENTS

1 small aubergine (eggplant)
2 courgettes (zucchini), thickly sliced
200g/7oz firm tofu, cubed
45ml/3 tbsp dark soy sauce
2–3 garlic cloves, crushed
10ml/2 tsp sesame seeds
1 red (bell) pepper, deseeded and sliced
1 onion, finely chopped
150ml/¼ pint/⅔ cup vegetable stock
3 firm ripe tomatoes, skinned, deseeded
and quartered
15ml/1 tbsp chopped fresh mixed herbs
225g/8oz dried penne
salt and ground black pepper
crusty bread, to serve

SERVES 6

1 Wash and cut the aubergine into
2.5cm/1in cubes. Put into a colander with
the courgettes, sprinkle with salt and
leave to drain for 30 minutes. Rinse
thoroughly, drain and set aside.

2 Mix the tofu with the soy sauce,
1 crushed garlic clove and the sesame
seeds. Cover and leave to marinate for
30 minutes.

NUTRITIONAL NOTES

Per portion:

Energy	208Kcals/873kJ
Total fat	3.7g
Saturated fat	0.5g
Cholesterol	0mg
Fibre	3.9g

4 Meanwhile cook the pasta in a large
pan of boiling salted water, according to
the packet instructions, until tender or
al dente. Drain thoroughly. Toss the pasta
with the vegetable mixture, the tofu and
the marinade. Transfer to a shallow
25cm/10in square ovenproof dish and
cook under a hot grill (broiler) until
lightly toasted. Transfer the bake to a
serving dish and serve immediately with
fresh crusty bread.

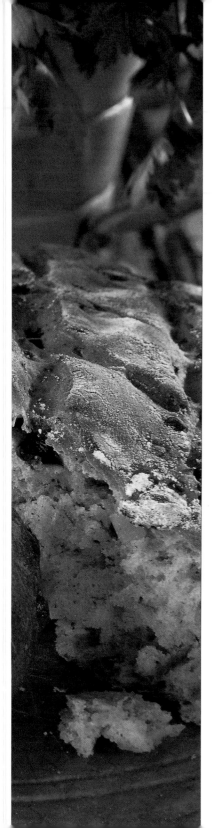

BREADS

It's hard to beat the AROMA *of freshly baked bread and once you've mastered the basic techniques it's* EASY *to make your own* BREAD. *We bring you a selection of Italian breads ideal for breakfast, brunch or a picnic alfresco. Choose from traditional* CIABATTA *and Focaccia breads, Olive and Oregano Bread, Sun-dried* TOMATO *Breadsticks or, for a slightly sweet bread, try the tempting Italian* CHOCOLATE *Bread.*

OLIVE AND OREGANO BREAD

This tasty Italian bread is an excellent low-fat accompaniment to all salads and is particularly good served warm.

INGREDIENTS
300ml/¹/2 pint/1¹/4 cups warm water
5ml/1 tsp dried yeast
pinch of sugar
15ml/1 tbsp olive oil
1 onion, chopped
450g/1lb/4 cups strong white bread flour,
plus extra for dusting
5ml/1 tsp salt
1.5ml/¹/4 tsp ground black pepper
50g/2oz/¹/2 cup pitted black olives,
roughly chopped
15ml/1 tbsp black olive paste
15ml/1 tbsp chopped
fresh oregano
15ml/1 tbsp chopped
fresh parsley

MAKES 1 LOAF, SERVES 8

1 Put half the warm water in a jug. Sprinkle the yeast on top. Add the sugar, mix well and leave for 10 minutes.

NUTRITIONAL NOTES
Per portion:

Energy	211Kcals/896kJ
Total fat	2.8g
Saturated fat	0.4g
Cholesterol	0mg
Fibre	2g

2 Heat the oil in a frying pan and fry the onion until golden brown, stirring occasionally. Remove the pan from the heat and set aside.

3 Sift the flour into a mixing bowl with the salt and pepper. Make a well in the centre. Add the yeast mixture, the fried onions (with the oil), the olives, olive paste, oregano, parsley and remaining water. Gradually incorporate the flour and mix to a soft dough, adding a little extra water if necessary.

4 Turn the dough out on to a lightly floured surface and knead for 5 minutes until smooth and elastic. Place in a mixing bowl, cover with a damp dish towel and leave to rise in a warm place for about 2 hours until the dough has doubled in bulk. Lightly grease a baking sheet and set aside.

5 Turn the dough out on to a lightly floured surface and knead again for a few minutes. Shape into a 20cm/8in round and place on the prepared baking sheet. Using a sharp knife, make criss-cross cuts over the top of the dough. Cover and leave in a warm place for 30 minutes until well risen. Preheat the oven to 220°C/425°F/Gas 7.

6 Dust the loaf with a little flour. Bake in the oven for 10 minutes then lower the oven temperature to 200°C/400°F/Gas 6. Bake for a further 20 minutes, or until the loaf sounds hollow when it is tapped underneath. Transfer to a wire rack to cool. Serve the bread warm or cold in slices or wedges.

ROSEMARY AND SEA SALT FOCACCIA

Focaccia is an appetizing Italian flat bread made with olive oil.
Here it is given added flavour with rosemary and coarse sea salt.

INGREDIENTS

350g/12oz/3 cups plain (all-purpose) flour
2.5ml/1/2 tsp salt
10ml/2 tsp easy-blend (rapid-rise)
dried yeast
about 250ml/8fl oz/1 cup lukewarm water
45ml/3 tbsp olive oil
1 small red onion
leaves from 1 large fresh rosemary sprig
5ml/1 tsp coarse sea salt
oil, for greasing

MAKES 1 LOAF, SERVES 8

1 Sift the flour and salt into a mixing bowl. Stir in the yeast, then make a well in the middle of the dry ingredients.

2 Pour in the water and 30ml/2 tbsp of the oil. Mix well to make a dough, adding a little more water if the mixture seems too dry.

3 Turn the dough out on to a lightly floured surface and knead it for about 10 minutes until smooth and elastic.

4 Place the dough in a greased bowl, cover and leave to rise in a warm place for about 1 hour until doubled in bulk. Knock back (punch down) and knead the dough on a floured surface for 2–3 minutes.

5 Preheat the oven to 220°C/425°F/Gas 7 and grease a baking sheet. Roll the dough to a circle 1cm/1/2in thick, transfer to the baking sheet and brush with remaining oil.

6 Halve the onion and chop it into thin slices. Press the slices lightly over the dough, with the rosemary and sea salt.

7 Using a finger, make deep indentations in the dough. Cover the surface with oiled clear film (plastic wrap), then leave to rise in a warm place for 30 minutes. Remove and discard the clear film and bake the loaf in the oven for 25–30 minutes until golden. Transfer to a wire rack to cool. Serve in slices or wedges.

COOK'S TIP

Use flavoured olive oil, such as chilli or herb oil, for extra flavour. Wholemeal (whole-wheat) flour or a mixture of wholemeal and white flour works well with this recipe.

NUTRITIONAL NOTES

Per portion:

Energy	191Kcals/807kJ
Total fat	4.72g
Saturated fat	0.68g
Cholesterol	0mg
Fibre	1.46g

SAFFRON FOCACCIA

**A dazzling yellow bread with a distinctive flavour, this saffron focaccia
makes a tasty snack or accompaniment.**

INGREDIENTS

FOR THE DOUGH
pinch of saffron threads
150ml/¹/4 pint/²/3 cup boiling water
225g/8oz/2 cups plain (all-purpose) flour
2.5ml/¹/2 tsp salt
5ml/1 tsp easy-blend (rapid-rise)
dried yeast
15ml/1 tbsp olive oil

FOR THE TOPPING
2 garlic cloves, sliced
1 red onion, cut into thin wedges
fresh rosemary sprigs
12 black olives, pitted and
coarsely chopped
15ml/1 tbsp olive oil

MAKES 1 LOAF, SERVES 10

1 Make the dough. In a jug (cup), infuse
the saffron in the boiling water. Leave
until cooled to lukewarm.

2 Place the flour, salt, yeast and olive oil
in a food processor. Turn the processor on
and gradually add the saffron and its
liquid until the dough forms a ball.

3 Transfer the dough on to a lightly
floured work surface and knead for
10–15 minutes until smooth and elastic.
Place in a bowl, cover and leave to rise in
a warm place for about 30–40 minutes,
until doubled in bulk. Lightly grease a
baking sheet and set aside.

4 Knock back (punch down) the risen
dough on a lightly floured surface and roll
out into an oval shape about 1cm/¹/2in
thick. Place on the prepared baking sheet
and leave to rise in a warm place for
20–30 minutes.

5 Preheat the oven to 200°C/400°F/
Gas 6. Use your fingers to press small
indentations in the dough.

6 Cover the dough with the topping
ingredients, brush lightly with the olive
oil, and bake the loaf in the oven for
about 25 minutes or until it sounds hollow
when tapped underneath. Transfer to a
wire rack to cool. Serve the focaccia in
slices or wedges.

VARIATION
You might like to experiment with
different topping ingredients for this
bread. Green olives and sun-dried
tomatoes are two others you could try.

NUTRITIONAL NOTES
Per portion:

Energy	177Kcals/754kJ
Total fat	4.7g
Saturated fat	0.7g
Cholesterol	0mg
Fibre	1.5g

ONION FOCACCIA
—

This typical Italian pizza-like flat bread is characterized by its soft dimpled surface. This
focaccia is flavoured with red onions and makes a tasty low-fat supper or snack.

INGREDIENTS
*675g/1½lb/6 cups strong white
bread flour
2.5ml/½ tsp salt
2.5ml/½ tsp caster (superfine) sugar
15ml/1 tbsp easy-blend (rapid-rise)
dried yeast
45ml/3 tbsp extra virgin olive oil
450ml/¾ pint/scant 2 cups hand-
hot water*

TO FINISH
*2 red onions, thinly sliced
15ml/1 tbsp extra virgin olive oil
15ml/1 tbsp coarse salt*

MAKES 2 LOAVES, SERVES 12

1 Sift the flour, salt and sugar into a large
bowl. Stir in the yeast, oil and water and
mix to a dough using a round-bladed
knife, adding a little extra water if the
dough is dry.

2 Turn the dough out on to a lightly
floured surface and knead for about
10 minutes until smooth and elastic. Put
the dough in a clean, lightly oiled bowl
and cover with clear film (plastic wrap).
Leave to rise in a warm place until
doubled in bulk.

3 Place two 25cm/10in plain metal flan
rings on baking sheets. Oil the sides of
the rings and the baking sheets.

4 Preheat the oven to 200°C/400°F/Gas 6.
Halve the dough and roll each piece of
dough into a 25cm/10in round. Press into
the prepared flan rings, cover with a
damp dish towel and leave to rise in a
warm place for 30 minutes.

NUTRITIONAL NOTES
Per portion:

Energy	231Kcals/975kJ
Total fat	4.4g
Saturated fat	0.6g
Cholesterol	0mg
Fibre	1.9g

5 Using a finger, make deep holes, about
2.5cm/1in apart, in the dough. Cover and
leave for a further 20 minutes.

6 To finish, scatter the dough with the
onions and drizzle over the oil. Sprinkle
with the salt, then a little cold water, to
stop a crust from forming.

7 Bake in the oven for about 25 minutes
until golden, sprinkling with water again
during cooking. Transfer to a wire rack to
cool. Serve in slices or wedges.

COOK'S TIP
When buying onions, look for ones
with dry, papery skins. To slice them,
cut a slice from the top and remove
the skin. Halve lengthways and slice
each half separately.

SAFFRON AND BASIL BREADSTICKS
—

Saffron lends its delicate aroma and flavour, as well as rich yellow colour, to these tasty breadsticks, ideal as a low-fat accompaniment, snack or nibble.

INGREDIENTS
generous pinch of saffron threads
30ml/2 tbsp hot water
450g/1lb/4 cups strong white bread flour
5ml/1 tsp salt
10ml/2 tsp easy-blend (rapid-rise) dried yeast
300ml/¹/2 pint/1¹/4 cups lukewarm water
45ml/3 tbsp olive oil
45ml/3 tbsp chopped fresh basil

MAKES 32

3 Add the oil and basil and continue to mix to form a soft dough.

6 Knock back (punch down) and knead on a floured surface for 2–3 minutes.

1 In a small bowl, infuse the saffron threads in the hot water for 10 minutes.

4 Knead the dough on a lightly floured surface for about 10 minutes until smooth and elastic.

7 Preheat the oven to 220°C/425°F/Gas 7. Lightly grease two baking sheets and set aside. Divide the dough into 32 even pieces and shape into long sticks. Place them well apart on the prepared baking sheets, then leave them for a further 15–20 minutes until they become puffy. Bake in the oven for about 15 minutes until crisp and golden. Transfer to a wire rack to cool. Serve warm or cold.

5 Place in a greased bowl, cover with clear film (plastic wrap) and leave to rise in a warm place for about 1 hour until the dough has doubled in bulk.

2 Sift the flour and salt into a large mixing bowl. Stir in the yeast, then make a well in the centre of the dry ingredients. Pour in the lukewarm water and saffron liquid and start to mix a little.

COOK'S TIP
Use powdered saffron if saffron threads are not available. Turmeric is an inexpensive alternative: it imparts a lovely gold colour, but its flavour is not as delicate.

NUTRITIONAL NOTES
Per portion:

Energy	59Kcals/249kJ
Total fat	1.3g
Saturated fat	1.17g
Cholesterol	0mg
Fibre	0.4g

SUN-DRIED TOMATO BREADSTICKS
—

Once you've tried this delicious and simple recipe you'll never buy manufactured breadsticks again. Serve with a low-fat dip or with low-fat cheese to end a meal.

INGREDIENTS

225g/8oz/2 cups plain (all-purpose) flour
2.5ml/1/2 tsp salt
7.5ml/11/2 tsp easy-blend (rapid-rise)
dried yeast
5ml/1 tsp honey
5ml/1 tsp olive oil
150ml/1/4 pint/2/3 cup warm water
6 halves sun-dried tomatoes in olive oil,
drained and chopped
15ml/1 tbsp skimmed milk
10ml/2 tsp poppy seeds

MAKES 16

1 Place the flour, salt and yeast in a food processor. Add the honey and olive oil and, with the processor running, gradually pour in the water. Stop adding water as soon as the dough starts to cling together. Process for a further 1 minute. Turn the dough out on to a lightly floured surface. Knead for 3–4 minutes until smooth and elastic.

NUTRITIONAL NOTES
Per portion:

Energy	54Kcals/228kJ
Total fat	0.8g
Saturated fat	0.1g
Cholesterol	0.02mg
Fibre	0.5g

2 Once the dough is very smooth, knead in the chopped sun-dried tomatoes. Form the dough into a large ball and place in a lightly oiled bowl. Leave to rest for 5 minutes. Lightly oil a baking sheet and set aside. Preheat the oven to 150°C/300°F/Gas 2.

3 Divide the dough into 16 equal pieces and roll each piece into a 28cm × 1cm/11in × 1/2in long stick. Place on the prepared baking sheet and leave to rise in a warm place for 15 minutes.

4 Brush the sticks with milk and sprinkle with poppy seeds. Bake in the oven for 30 minutes. Place on a wire rack to cool.

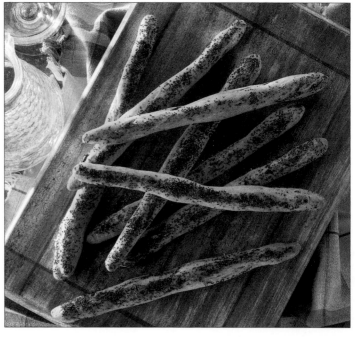

CHOCOLATE BREAD

This slightly sweet chocolate bread from Italy is often served with a little creamy mascarpone as a special dessert. The dark chocolate pieces add texture to this light loaf.

3 Turn the dough out on to a lightly floured surface and knock back (punch down). Knead in the chocolate, then cover with oiled clear film. Leave to rest for 5 minutes.

4 Shape the dough into a round and place in the prepared tin. Cover with lightly oiled clear film and leave to rise, in a warm place, for 45 minutes, or until doubled in bulk.

5 Preheat the oven to 220°C/425°F/Gas 7. Bake in the oven for 10 minutes, then reduce the oven temperature to 190°C/375°F/Gas 5 and bake for a further 25–30 minutes. Brush the hot bread with melted butter and transfer to a wire rack to cool. Serve in slices.

INGREDIENTS

350g/12oz/3 cups unbleached strong white
bread flour
25ml/1^{1}/2 tbsp cocoa powder
2.5ml/^{1}/2 tsp salt
25g/1oz/2 tbsp caster (superfine) sugar
15g/^{1}/2oz fresh yeast
250ml/8fl oz/1 cup lukewarm water
25g/1oz/2 tbsp butter, softened
75g/3oz plain (semi-sweet) chocolate,
coarsely chopped
15ml/1 tbsp melted butter, for brushing

MAKES 1 LOAF, SERVES 12

NUTRITIONAL NOTES

Per portion:

Energy	154Kcals/651kJ
Total fat	4.8g
Saturated fat	2.8g
Cholesterol	7.4mg
Fibre	1.0g

1 Lightly grease a 15cm/6in deep round cake tin (pan). Set aside. Sift the flour, cocoa and salt together in a large bowl. Stir in the sugar. Make a well in the centre.

2 Cream the yeast with 60ml/4 tbsp of the water, then stir in the remaining water. Add to the centre of the flour mixture and mix to a dough. Knead in the butter, then turn out and knead on a lightly floured surface until smooth and elastic. Place in an oiled bowl, cover with clear film (plastic wrap) and leave to rise, in a warm place, for 1 hour, or until doubled in bulk.

VARIATION

You can also bake this in one large or two small rounds on a baking sheet.

DESSERTS
AND
BAKES

Desserts provide the flavourful FINALE *to a meal, and we include a collection of delectable* HOT *and cold Italian desserts, all of which are* LOW *in fat too! Select from delights such as classic* ZABAGLIONE, *Nectarines with Ricotta and Spice,* SORBETS *such as* MANGO *and Lime Sorbet or Watermelon Sorbet, and bakes such as Chocolate* AMARETTI *or Biscotti.*

STRAWBERRY CONCHIGLIE SALAD

This is a divinely decadent Italian low-fat dessert, laced with liqueur and luscious raspberry sauce, for all the family to enjoy.

INGREDIENTS

175g/6oz/1¹/₂ cups dried conchiglie
a little salt
225g/8oz fresh or frozen raspberries,
thawed if frozen
15–30ml/1–2 tbsp caster (superfine) sugar
lemon juice
450g/1lb small fresh strawberries
15g/¹/₂oz flaked (sliced) almonds
45ml/3 tbsp kirsch

SERVES 4

1 Cook the pasta in a large pan of boiling lightly salted water, according to the packet instructions, until tender or al dente. Drain well and set aside to cool.

2 Purée the raspberries in a blender or food processor and press through a sieve (strainer) to remove the seeds. Discard the seeds.

3 Add the sugar to the raspberry purée, then place in a pan and simmer for 5–6 minutes, stirring occasionally. Add lemon juice to taste. Remove the pan from the heat and set aside to cool.

4 Hull the strawberries and halve if necessary. Toss with the pasta and transfer to a serving bowl.

NUTRITIONAL NOTES
Per portion:

Energy	203Kcals/861kJ
Total fat	1.8g
Saturated fat	0.2g
Cholesterol	0mg
Fibre	3.4g

5 Spread the almonds out on a baking sheet and toast under a hot grill (broiler) until golden. Set aside to cool.

6 Stir the kirsch into the raspberry sauce and pour over the pasta salad. Scatter the toasted almonds over the top of the salad and serve.

COOK'S TIP
Like all soft fruit, strawberries and raspberries should be used as soon as possible after they are picked. Wash them very gently and use immediately.

VARIATION
You might like to try making sweet pasta salads with other types of soft fruit such as blackberries and loganberries.

FRESH FIG, APPLE AND DATE DESSERT

—

Sweet Mediterranean figs and dates combine especially well with crisp dessert apples to create this appetizing low-fat dessert. A hint of almond serves to unite the flavours.

INGREDIENTS
6 large apples
juice of 1/2 lemon
175g/6oz fresh dates
25g/1oz white marzipan
5ml/1 tsp orange flower water
60ml/4 tbsp low-fat natural (plain) yogurt
4 ripe green or purple fresh figs
4 whole almonds, toasted

SERVES 4

1 Core the apples. Slice them thinly, then cut into thin matchsticks. Put into a bowl, sprinkle with lemon juice to keep them white and set aside.

2 Remove and discard the stones (pits) from the dates and cut the flesh into thin strips, then combine with the apple slices. Toss to mix.

3 In a small bowl, soften the marzipan with the orange flower water and combine this with the yogurt. Mix well.

4 Pile the mixed apples and dates into the centre of four plates. Remove and discard the stem from each of the figs and cut the fruit into quarters without cutting right through the base. Squeeze the base with the thumb and forefinger of each hand to open up the fruit.

NUTRITIONAL NOTES
Per portion:

Energy	178Kcals/751kJ
Total fat	2.3g
Saturated fat	0.2g
Cholesterol	0.5mg
Fibre	4.4g

5 Place a fig in the centre of each apple and date salad, spoon in some yogurt filling and decorate each portion with a toasted almond. Serve.

COOK'S TIPS
• Figs are at their best straight off the tree when they are perfectly ripe. Bear in mind that ripe figs are extremely delicate and do not travel well, so take great care not to squash them on the way home. If you buy under-ripe figs, they can be kept at room temperature for a day or two until the skin softens, but they will never develop the fine flavour of tree-ripened figs. Ripe figs should be eaten on the day they are bought.
• When choosing fresh dates, select those that are fat and shiny, with skins that are golden and smooth. You may wish to remove the skin by squeezing the stem end. Most figs, however, have thin skins that are edible.

VARIATION
For a true Mediterranean touch, use fresh fig or vine leaves, if available, to decorate the serving plates for this dessert.

BAKED FRUIT COMPOTE

——

Mixed dried fruits, combined with fruit juice and spices, then oven-baked, make a nutritious and warming Italian-style winter dessert.

INGREDIENTS

115g/4oz/²/3 cup ready-to-eat dried figs
*115g/4oz/¹/2 cup ready-to-eat
dried apricots*
*50g/2oz/¹/2 cup ready-to-eat dried
apple rings*
50g/2oz/¹/4 cup ready-to-eat prunes
50g/2oz/¹/2 cup ready-to-eat dried pears
50g/2oz/¹/2 cup ready-to-eat dried peaches
*300ml/¹/2 pint/1¹/4 cups unsweetened
apple juice*
*300ml/2oz/¹/4 pint/1¹/4 cups unsweetened
orange juice*
6 cloves
1 cinnamon stick
*toasted flaked (sliced) almonds,
to decorate (optional)*

SERVES 6

1 Preheat the oven to 180°C/350°F/Gas 4. Place the figs, apricots, apple rings, prunes, pears and peaches in a shallow ovenproof dish and stir to mix.

2 Mix together the apple and orange juices and pour over the fruit. Add the cloves and cinnamon stick and stir gently to mix.

3 Bake in the oven for about 30 minutes until the fruit mixture is hot, stirring once or twice during cooking. Remove from the oven, set aside and leave to soak for 20 minutes, then remove and discard the cloves and cinnamon stick.

4 Spoon into serving bowls and serve warm or cold, decorated with toasted flaked almonds, if you like.

NUTRITIONAL NOTES
Per portion:

Energy	174Kcals/744kJ
Total fat	0.8g
Saturated fat	0.05g
Cholesterol	0mg
Fibre	5.16g

MANGO YOGURT ICE

——

Serve this delicious mango yogurt ice in scoops for a popular and low-fat family dessert.

INGREDIENTS

450g/1lb ripe mango flesh, chopped
300ml/¹/2 pint/1¹/4 cups low-fat peach yogurt
*150ml/¹/4 pint/²/3 cup Greek (US strained
plain) yogurt*
*150ml/¹/4 pint/²/3 cup low-fat natural
(plain) yogurt*
*25–50g/1–2oz/2–4 tbsp caster (superfine)
sugar*
fresh mint sprigs, to decorate

SERVES 6

1 Blend the mango flesh in a blender or food processor and blend until smooth. Transfer to a bowl. Mix in all three yogurts.

2 Add enough of the sugar to sweeten to taste and stir to mix. Pour into a shallow, plastic container. Cover and freeze for 1¹/2–2 hours until it is mushy in consistency. Turn the mixture into a chilled bowl and beat until smooth.

3 Return the mixture to the plastic container, cover and freeze until firm. Transfer the ice to the refrigerator about 30 minutes before serving to allow it to soften a little. Serve in scoops, decorated with fresh mint sprigs.

NUTRITIONAL NOTES
Per portion:

Energy	155Kcals/655kJ
Total fat	2.9g
Saturated fat	1.7g
Cholesterol	6.5mg
Fibre	2.17g

LEMON GRANITA

Nothing is more refreshing on a hot summer's day than an Italian fat-free fresh lemon granita.
Try making a lime version as well.

INGREDIENTS
475ml/16fl oz/2 cups water
115g/4oz/1/2 cup sugar
2 large lemons

SERVES 4

NUTRITIONAL NOTES
Per portion:

Energy	114Kcals/488kJ
Total fat	0g
Saturated fat	0g
Cholesterol	0mg
Fibre	0g

1 In a large pan, heat the water and the sugar together over a low heat until the sugar dissolves. Bring to the boil, stirring occasionally. Remove the pan from the heat and set aside to cool.

2 Finely grate the rind from 1 lemon, then squeeze the juice from both. Stir the grated lemon rind and juice into the sugar syrup. Pour it into a shallow plastic container or freezer tray, and freeze until it is solid.

3 Plunge the bottom of the frozen container or tray in very hot water for a few seconds. Turn the frozen mixture out into a bowl and chop it into large chunks.

4 Place the mixture in a blender or food processor fitted with metal blades, and process until it forms small crystals. Spoon the granita into serving glasses and serve immediately.

COFFEE GRANITA

Espresso coffee adds a delicious flavour to this appetizing fat-free Italian-style dessert.

INGREDIENTS
475ml/16fl oz/2 cups water
115g/4oz/1/2 cup sugar
250ml/8fl oz/1 cup very strong espresso coffee, cooled

SERVES 4

1 Heat the water and sugar together in a pan until the sugar dissolves. Bring to the boil, stirring occasionally. Remove the pan from the heat and set aside to cool.

2 Stir the cooled coffee and the sugar syrup together. Pour the mixture into a shallow, plastic container and freeze until solid. Plunge the bottom of the frozen container in very hot water for a few seconds. Turn the frozen mixture out into a bowl and chop it into large chunks.

3 Place the mixture in a blender or food processor fitted with metal blades, and process until it forms small crystals. Spoon the granita into tall serving glasses and serve.

COOK'S TIP
If not served immediately, the granita can be frozen again.

NUTRITIONAL NOTES
Per portion:

Energy	115Kcals/488kJ
Total fat	0g
Saturated fat	0g
Cholesterol	0mg
Fibre	0g

WATERMELON SORBET

—

A slice of this refreshing Italian fruit sorbet is the perfect way to cool down on a hot sunny day.
It also makes an excellent summer appetizer.

INGREDIENTS

1/2 small watermelon, weighing about
1kg/2¼lb
75g/3oz/½ cup caster (superfine) sugar
60ml/4 tbsp cranberry juice or water
30ml/2 tbsp lemon juice
fresh mint sprigs, to decorate

SERVES 6

1 Cut the watermelon into six equal-sized wedges. Scoop out the pink flesh from each wedge, discarding the seeds but reserving the shell.

2 Line a freezerproof bowl, about the same size as the melon, with clear film (plastic wrap). Arrange the melon skins in the bowl to re-form the shell, fitting them together snugly so that there are no gaps. Put in the freezer.

3 Put the sugar and cranberry juice or water in a pan and stir over a low heat until the sugar dissolves. Bring to the boil, then reduce the heat and simmer for 5 minutes. Remove the pan from the heat and set aside to cool.

4 Put the melon flesh and lemon juice in a blender or food processor and blend to a smooth purée. Pour into a bowl, stir in the sugar syrup, then pour into a freezer-proof container. Freeze the mixture for 3–3½ hours, or until slushy.

NUTRITIONAL NOTES

Per portion:

Energy	101Kcals/434kJ
Total fat	0.5g
Saturated fat	0.2g
Cholesterol	0mg
Fibre	0.2g

5 Tip the sorbet into a chilled freezerproof bowl and whisk well to break up the ice crystals. Return to the freezer for a further 30 minutes. Whisk again, then tip into the melon shell and freeze until solid.

6 Remove the sorbet from the freezer and leave to stand at room temperature for 15 minutes. Take the melon out of the bowl and cut into wedges with a warmed sharp knife. Serve decorated with fresh mint sprigs.

COOK'S TIP

If preferred, this pretty pink sorbet can be served scooped into balls. Do this before the mixture is completely frozen and re-freeze the balls on a baking sheet, ready to serve.

ICED ORANGES

—

The ultimate virtually fat-free treat – these delectable orange sorbets served in fruit shells create a light and refreshing flavourful dessert.

INGREDIENTS

150g/5oz/²/3 cup sugar
juice of 1 lemon
14 oranges
8 fresh bay leaves, to decorate

SERVES 8

1 Put the sugar in a heavy pan. Add half the lemon juice, then add 120ml/4fl oz/ ½ cup water. Cook over a low heat until the sugar has dissolved, stirring. Bring to the boil and boil for 2–3 minutes until the syrup is clear. Remove the pan from the heat and set aside.

2 Slice the tops off eight of the oranges to make "hats". Scoop out the flesh of the oranges and reserve. Freeze the empty orange shells and "hats" until required.

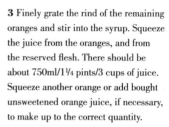

3 Finely grate the rind of the remaining oranges and stir into the syrup. Squeeze the juice from the oranges, and from the reserved flesh. There should be about 750ml/1¼ pints/3 cups of juice. Squeeze another orange or add bought unsweetened orange juice, if necessary, to make up to the correct quantity.

4 Stir the orange juice and remaining lemon juice with 90ml/6 tbsp water into the syrup. Taste, adding more lemon juice or sugar as desired. Pour the mixture into a shallow freezerproof container and freeze for 3 hours.

5 Turn the orange sorbet mixture into a chilled bowl and whisk thoroughly to break up the ice crystals. Return to the container and freeze for a further 4 hours, until firm, but not solid.

6 Pack the frozen mixture into the hollowed-out orange shells, mounding it up, and set the "hats" on top. Freeze the filled sorbet shells until ready to serve. Just before serving, push a skewer into the tops of the "hats" and push in a bay leaf, to decorate.

NUTRITIONAL NOTES

Per portion:

Energy	139Kcals/593kJ
Total fat	0.17g
Saturated fat	0g
Cholesterol	0mg
Fibre	3g

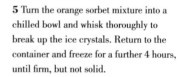

ITALIAN FRUIT SALAD AND ICE CREAM

If you visit Italy in the summer, you will find little pavement fruit shops selling small dishes of macerated soft fruits, which are delectable on their own, but also wonderful with low-fat ice cream.

INGREDIENTS

900g/2lb/8 cups mixed ripe soft fruits,
such as strawberries, raspberries,
loganberries, redcurrants, blueberries,
peaches, apricots, plums and melons
juice of 6–8 oranges
juice of 1 lemon
15ml/1 tbsp liquid pear and
apple concentrate
60ml/4 tbsp very low-fat fromage frais
30ml/2 tbsp orange-flavoured
liqueur (optional)
fresh mint sprigs, to decorate

SERVES 6

1 Prepare the fruit according to type. Cut it into reasonably small pieces, but not so small that the mixture becomes a mush.

2 Put the fruit in a serving bowl and pour over enough orange juice to cover. Add the lemon juice, stir gently to mix, cover and chill in the refrigerator for 2 hours.

3 Set half the macerated fruit aside to serve as it is. Purée the remainder in a blender or food processor. Pour the purée into a bowl.

4 Gently warm the pear and apple concentrate in a small pan and stir it into the fruit purée. Whip the fromage frais and fold it in to the fruit purée, then add the liqueur, if using.

NUTRITIONAL NOTES

Per portion:

Energy	60Kcals/254kJ
Total fat	0.2g
Saturated fat	0.01g
Cholesterol	0.1mg
Fibre	3.2g

5 Churn the mixture in an ice cream maker. Alternatively, place in a shallow freezerproof container and freeze it until ice crystals form around the edge. Beat the mixture in a chilled bowl until smooth. Repeat the process once or twice, then freeze until firm. Soften slightly in the refrigerator before serving in scoops. Decorate with mint sprigs and serve with the macerated fruit.

NECTARINE AMARETTO CAKE

—

Try this delicious Italian-style cake served with a little low-fat fromage frais for dessert, or serve it solo for an afternoon tea treat. The syrup makes it deliciously moist but not soggy.

INGREDIENTS
3 eggs, separated
*175g/6oz/generous ¾ cup caster
(superfine) sugar*
finely grated rind and juice of 1 lemon
50g/2oz/⅓ cup semolina
40g/1½ oz/⅓ cup ground almonds
25g/1oz/¼ cup plain (all-purpose) flour
*2 nectarines or peaches,
halved and stoned (pitted)*
*60ml/4 tbsp apricot glaze
(see Cook's Tip)*

FOR THE SYRUP
75g/3oz/6 tbsp caster (superfine) sugar
90ml/6 tbsp water
30ml/2 tbsp Amaretto liqueur

SERVES 10

1 Preheat the oven to 180°C/350°F/Gas 4. Lightly grease a 20cm/8in round loose-based cake tin (pan). Whisk the egg yolks, caster sugar, lemon rind and juice in a bowl until thick, pale and creamy. Fold in the semolina, almonds and flour.

2 Whisk the egg whites in a separate bowl until fairly stiff. Using a metal spoon, stir a generous spoonful of the whisked egg whites into the semolina mixture to lighten it, then fold in the remaining egg whites. Spoon the mixture into the prepared cake tin and then level the surface.

3 Bake in the oven for 30–35 minutes until the centre of the cake springs back when lightly pressed. Remove the cake from the oven and carefully loosen around the edge with a palette knife. Prick the top of the cake all over with a skewer and leave to cool slightly in the tin.

4 Meanwhile, make the syrup. Heat the sugar and water in a small pan, stirring until dissolved, then boil without stirring for 2 minutes. Stir in the Amaretto liqueur, then drizzle the syrup slowly over the top of the cake.

5 Remove the cake from the tin and place it on a serving plate. Slice the nectarines or peaches, arrange them over the top of the cake and brush with the warm apricot glaze. Serve warm or cold in slices.

COOK'S TIP
To make apricot glaze, place a few spoonfuls of apricot jam in a small pan along with a squeeze of lemon juice. Heat the jam, stirring until it is melted and runny. Pour the melted jam through a wire sieve (strainer) set over a bowl and stir the jam with a wooden spoon to help it go through. Discard the contents of the sieve. Keep the strained jam/glaze warm and use as required.

NUTRITIONAL NOTES
Per portion:

Energy	165Kcals/701kJ
Total fat	1.8g
Saturated fat	0.5g
Cholesterol	57mg
Fibre	0.4g

CHOCOLATE AMARETTI

These mouthwatering Italian chocolate amaretti are delicious served on their own
or with low-fat sorbet, mousse or zabaglione.

INGREDIENTS

150g/5oz/1 cup blanched whole almonds
90g/3¹/₂oz/¹/₂ cup caster (superfine) sugar
15ml/1 tbsp unsweetened cocoa powder
30ml/2 tbsp icing (confectioners') sugar
2 egg whites
pinch of cream of tartar
5ml/1 tsp almond extract
15g/¹/₂oz flaked (sliced) almonds,
to decorate

MAKES ABOUT 24

1 Preheat oven to 180°C/350°F/Gas 4.
Place the whole almonds on a small
baking sheet and bake in the oven for
10–12 minutes, stirring occasionally,
until the almonds are golden brown.
Remove from the oven and set aside to
cool to room temperature. Reduce the
oven temperature to 160°C/325°F/Gas 3.

2 Line a large baking sheet with non-
stick baking parchment or foil and set
aside. In a blender or food processor
fitted with a metal blade, process the
toasted almonds with 45g/1³/₄oz/¹/₄ cup
sugar until the almonds are finely ground
but not oily. Transfer to a medium bowl
and sift in the cocoa powder and icing
sugar; stir to mix. Set aside.

3 In a mixing bowl, beat the egg whites
and cream of tartar together, using an
electric mixer, until stiff peaks form.
Sprinkle in the remaining 45g/1³/₄oz/
¹/₄ cup sugar, a tablespoon at a time,
beating well after each addition, and
continue beating until the egg whites
are glossy and stiff. Beat in the
almond extract.

4 Sprinkle the almond-sugar mixture
over the whisked egg whites and gently
fold them in until just blended. Spoon
the mixture into a large piping (pastry)
bag fitted with a plain 1cm/¹/₂in nozzle.
Pipe the mixture into 4cm/1¹/₂in rounds
about 2.5cm/1in apart on the prepared
baking sheet.

5 Press a flaked almond into the centre of
each one and bake the amaretti in the
oven for 12–15 minutes or until they
appear crisp. Place the baking sheets
on a wire rack and leave to cool for
10 minutes. With a metal palette knife,
remove the amaretti and place on a wire
rack, then leave to cool completely. When
cool, store in an airtight container.

NUTRITIONAL NOTES
Per portion:

Energy	58Kcals/244kJ
Total fat	3.7g
Saturated fat	0.4g
Cholesterol	0mg
Fibre	0.6g

APRICOT AND ALMOND FINGERS

These moist apricot and almond fingers are an irresistible low-fat snack
or treat for all to enjoy.

2 Turn the mixture into the prepared tin, spread to the edges and sprinkle with the flaked almonds.

3 Bake in the oven for 30–35 minutes or until the centre of the cake springs back when lightly pressed. Turn out onto a wire rack and allow to cool. Remove and discard the paper, place the cake on a board and cut it into 18 slices with a sharp knife. Store in an airtight container.

INGREDIENTS
*225g/8oz/2 cups self-raising
(self-rising) flour
115g/4oz/⅔ cup light muscovado
(brown) sugar
50g/2oz/⅓ cup semolina
175g/6oz/1 cup ready-to-eat dried
apricots, chopped
2 eggs
30ml/2 tbsp malt extract
30ml/2 tbsp clear honey
60ml/4 tbsp skimmed milk
60ml/4 tbsp sunflower oil
few drops of almond extract
30ml/2 tbsp flaked (sliced) almonds*

MAKES 18

1 Preheat the oven to 160°C/325°F/Gas 3. Lightly grease and line a 28 × 18cm/11 × 7in shallow baking tin (pan) and set aside. Sift the flour into a bowl and add the sugar, semolina, dried apricots, eggs, malt extract, honey, milk, oil and almond extract. Mix well until smooth.

NUTRITIONAL NOTES
Per portion:

Energy	153Kcals/641kJ
Total fat	4.56g
Saturated fat	0.61g
Cholesterol	21.5mg
Fibre	1.27g

BISCOTTI

These delicious Italian biscuits are part-baked, sliced to reveal a feast of mixed nuts and then baked again until crisp and golden. They're perfect for rounding off a low-fat Italian meal.

INGREDIENTS

50g/2oz/¹/4 cup unsalted butter, softened
115g/4oz/¹/2 cup caster (superfine) sugar
175g/6oz/1¹/2 cups self-raising
(self-rising) flour
1.5ml/¹/4 tsp salt
10ml/2 tsp baking powder
5ml/1 tsp ground coriander
finely grated rind of 1 lemon
50g/2oz/¹/2 cup polenta
1 egg, lightly beaten
10ml/2 tsp brandy or orange-
flavour liqueur
50g/2oz/¹/2 cup unblanched almonds
50g/2oz/¹/2 cup pistachio nuts

MAKES 24

1 Preheat the oven to 160°C/325°F/Gas 3. Grease a baking sheet and set aside. Cream together the butter and sugar in a bowl.

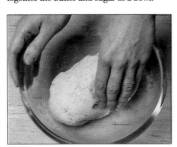

2 Sift the flour, salt, baking powder and coriander over the creamed mixture in the bowl. Add the lemon rind, polenta, egg and brandy or liqueur and mix together to make a soft dough.

COOK'S TIP

Use a sharp, serrated knife to slice the cooled biscotti in Step 4, otherwise they will crumble.

---

3 Add the nuts and mix until evenly combined. Halve the mixture. Shape each half of the dough into a flat sausage about 23cm/9in long and 6cm/2¹/2in wide. Place on the prepared baking sheet. Bake in the oven for about 30 minutes until risen and just firm. Remove from the oven and set aside to cool on a wire rack.

NUTRITIONAL NOTES
Per portion:

Energy	94Kcals/397kJ
Total fat	4.2g
Saturated fat	1.2g
Cholesterol	12.6mg
Fibre	0.2g

4 When cool, cut each sausage diagonally into 12 thin slices. Return to the baking sheet and bake in the oven for a further 10 minutes until crisp.

5 Transfer the biscotti to a wire rack to cool completely. Store in an airtight container for up to one week.

INDEX

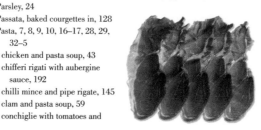